ULTIMATE

THE

NINJA
POSSIBLE COOKER PRO
COOKBOOK

GET YOUR
BONUS
100% FREE
SCAN THE QR CODE OR GO TO
https://sites.google.com/view/freebonusbooks

You don't need to enter any details

except your e-mail

GET YOUR FREE BONUS PASSWORD ON PAGE 28

Table of Contents

CHAPTER SEVEN

STEAM RECIPES

INTRODUCTION

Welcome to my Ninja Foodi Possible Cooker Pro Cookbook! This cookbook is your one-stop shop for delicious, easy-to-make recipes that you can create in your Ninja Foodi Possible Cooker Pro.

Whether you're a busy parent, a college student, or simply someone who loves to cook, the Ninja Foodi Possible Cooker Pro is a kitchen appliance that can help you make delicious meals quickly and easily. With its eight functions (slow cook, braise, steam, keep warm, bake, proof, saute/sear, and sous vide), the Ninja Foodi Possible Cooker Pro can do it all.

This cookbook provides you with a variety of recipes for each function of the cooker, so you can experiment and find new favorites. From classic comfort foods to healthy and creative dishes, there's something for everyone in this cookbook.

Here are just a few of the delicious recipes you'll find in this cookbook:

- **Slow Cook: Pork stew, Beef Stew, Salmon soup, and glazed chicken**

- **Braise: Red Wine Braised Beef, Pork Belly, and Lamb Tagine**

- **Steam: Fish and Vegetables**

- **Bake: Cakes and Breads**

- **Proof: Dough for bread and pizza**

- **Saute/Sear: Beef, Chicken, and Seafood**

- **Sous Vide: Pork belly, Salmon, and Lamb**

I hope you enjoy these recipes and find the Ninja Foodi Possible Cooker Pro to be a valuable addition to your kitchen. With this cookbook and your Ninja Foodi Possible Cooker Pro, you'll be able to make delicious meals that will impress your family and friends.

Happy cooking!

CHAPTER ONE

All about the Ninja Foodi Possible Cooker Pro

The Ninja Foodi Possible Cooker Pro is a versatile kitchen appliance designed to streamline your cooking experience. It offers eight distinct cooking functions, making it a multi-functional kitchen workhorse. Whether you want to slow cook soups, braise meat, keep food warm, proof bread dough, bake cake, sauté or sear, use sous vide techniques, or steam, this appliance has you covered. Its innovative features and user-friendly design make it a valuable addition to any kitchen, enabling you to prepare a wide range of dishes with ease and precision.

Ninja Foodi Possible Cooker Pro Cooking Functions

1. THE SLOW COOK FUNCTION

The slow cook function on the Ninja Foodi Possible Cooker Pro is a convenient way to prepare dishes that require long, low-temperature cooking.

How it works:

✓ Temperature Control: The slow cook function allows you to set the cooking temperature to a low and consistent level, typically between **170°F to 280°F (77°C to 138°C)**. This low and steady temperature is ideal for slow-cooking because it gradually breaks down tough cuts of meat and allows flavors to meld.

✓ Cooking Time: You can select the cooking time based on your recipe's requirements. Slow cooking often spans several hours, which is perfect for tenderizing meats, simmering stews, and developing rich, deep flavors.

✓ Versatile Cooking: With the slow cook function, you can prepare a wide range of dishes, including pulled pork, beef stew, chili, soups, and more. It's also great for making sauces, such as marinara or barbecue sauce, that benefit from long, slow simmering.

✓ Hands-Off Cooking: Once you've set the temperature and cooking time, the Ninja Foodi Possible Cooker Pro takes care of the rest. You can leave it unattended, making it a convenient option for busy individuals or when you want to prepare meals in advance.

✓ Tenderizing Meat: Slow cooking is excellent for tenderizing tough cuts of meat. The low temperature and extended cooking time allow collagen in the meat to break down, resulting in tender and flavorful dishes.

✓ Flavor Development: The slow cook function helps flavors meld and intensify over time, making your dishes taste even better as they simmer.

✓ Keep Warm Feature: After the slow cooking cycle is complete, the appliance often switches to a "keep warm" mode, ensuring your meal remains at a safe serving temperature until you're ready to enjoy it.

2. THE BRAISE FUNCTION

The braise function on the Ninja Foodi Possible Cooker Pro is a versatile cooking option that's ideal for tenderizing and flavoring various ingredients, particularly meats and vegetables.

How it works:

✓ Temperature Control: The braise function allows you to cook at a moderate and consistent temperature, typically between **275°F to 350°F (135°C to 177°C)**. This temperature range is ideal for braising because it promotes browning and caramelization while slowly breaking down tough fibers in the ingredients.

✓ Cooking Method: Braising is a cooking technique that combines searing and slow cooking in a flavorful liquid. It involves first searing the ingredient (e.g., meat), then simmered or roasted in a flavorful liquid, such as broth, wine, or sauce, at a low and steady temperature.

✓ Versatility: The braise function is excellent for preparing dishes like pot roast, coq au vin, beef bourguignon, and osso buco. It's also suitable for vegetables like Brussels sprouts or leeks, which become tender and infused with flavor when braised.

✓ Flavor Infusion: During the braising process, the ingredient absorbs the flavors of the cooking liquid and aromatic ingredients (e.g., onions, garlic, herbs) in the pot. This results in a deeply flavorful and succulent dish.

✓ Tenderizing: Braising is particularly effective at tenderizing tough cuts of meat. The slow cooking in the liquid helps break down collagen and connective tissues, resulting in melt-in-your-mouth tenderness.

✓ Brown Crust: The initial searing of the ingredient creates a flavorful brown crust that adds depth and texture to the dish.

✓ One-Pot Convenience: The Ninja Foodi Possible Cooker Pro's braise function allows you to sear and braise in the same pot, minimizing cleanup and maximizing flavor.

✓ Customization: You can customize the cooking time and temperature based on your specific recipe and desired results. This flexibility ensures that your braised dishes turn out perfectly.

3. THE KEEP WARM FUNCTION

The "Keep Warm" function on the Ninja Foodi Possible Cooker Pro is a valuable feature that helps maintain the temperature of your cooked food at a safe and serving-ready level without overcooking or cooling down too quickly.

How it works:

✓ Temperature Maintenance: The Keep Warm function operates at a low and consistent temperature, typically around **165°F (74°C)**. This temperature range is designed to keep your cooked food warm without continuing to cook it, which is crucial for preventing overcooking and maintaining food quality.

✓ Use After Cooking: Once you've completed the cooking cycle for a particular dish using one of the other functions (e.g., slow cooking, braising, baking), you can switch to the Keep Warm function. It helps ensure that your food remains at a safe and ready-to-serve temperature until you're ready to eat.

- ✓ Preventing Foodborne Illness: Keeping food at a safe temperature is essential to prevent foodborne illnesses. The Keep Warm function maintains food within the safe temperature range (above 140°F or 60°C) required to inhibit the growth of harmful bacteria.

- ✓ Convenient for Serving: This function is particularly useful when you have guests or family members with varying meal schedules. It allows you to prepare a meal in advance and keep it warm until everyone is ready to eat, eliminating the need for reheating and preserving the food's freshness.

- ✓ Ideal for Buffets and Potlucks: If you're hosting a buffet-style meal or attending a potluck, the Keep Warm function ensures that your dishes remain at a safe and enjoyable temperature throughout the event.

- ✓ Safety Timer: Some appliances with a Keep Warm function have an automatic timer that turns off the function after a set period (e.g., 2 hours) to prevent food from sitting at warm temperatures for an extended duration, which can impact quality and safety.

4. THE PROOF FUNCTION

The "Proof" function on the Ninja Foodi Possible Cooker Pro is designed primarily for proofing bread dough, making it rise and expand before baking.

How it works:

- ✓ Temperature Control: The Proof function maintains a low and consistent temperature, typically around **90°F to 100°F (32°C to 38°C)**. This temperature range is ideal for activating yeast and facilitating the fermentation process required for bread dough to rise.

- ✓ Fermentation: Proofing is a crucial step in breadmaking. During this phase, yeast cells consume sugars and produce carbon dioxide gas and alcohol. The gas gets trapped in the dough, causing it to expand and rise, which results in a lighter, fluffier bread with an airy texture.

- ✓ Dough Preparation: After kneading your bread dough, you can place it in a bowl or container, cover it with a damp cloth or plastic wrap, and then use the Proof function to create the optimal environment for fermentation.

✓ Ideal for Homemade Bread: This function is particularly useful for home bakers who want to create homemade bread, rolls, or other yeast-leavened baked goods. It ensures consistent and reliable results by providing the right temperature and humidity for proofing.

✓ Customization: The Ninja Foodi Possible Cooker Pro often allows you to customize the proofing time based on your recipe's requirements. Different bread recipes may call for varying proofing durations, and this function can accommodate those needs.

✓ Versatility: While primarily used for bread dough, the Proof function can also be employed for other yeast-based recipes like pizza dough, cinnamon rolls, and even some pastry doughs that benefit from controlled proofing.

✓ Hands-Free Proofing: Once you've set the Proof function and placed your dough inside, the appliance takes care of maintaining the ideal temperature and humidity, allowing you to attend to other tasks while your dough rises.

✓ Consistent Results: Using the Proof function ensures that your bread rises evenly, resulting in a well-structured and flavorful final product.

✓ Enhanced Flavor and Texture: Proper proofing not only contributes to the volume of the bread but also enhances its flavor and texture, making it more enjoyable to eat.

5. THE BAKE FUNCTION

The "Bake" function on the Ninja Foodi Possible Cooker Pro is a versatile cooking option designed for a wide range of baked dishes, both savory and sweet.

How it works:

✓ Temperature Control: The Bake function allows you to set and maintain a specific cooking temperature, which typically ranges from **250°F to 450°F (121°C to 232°C)**, depending on the recipe's requirements. This temperature control is crucial for achieving the desired texture and browning in your baked goods.

✓ Even Heat Distribution: The appliance's heating elements are strategically placed to ensure even heat distribution throughout the cooking chamber, promoting consistent results.

✓ Baking Modes: Depending on the model of the Ninja Foodi Possible Cooker Pro, you may have access to different baking modes, such as convection baking, air frying, or traditional baking. These modes can be selected based on the type of dish you're preparing, allowing for more precise cooking.

✓ Versatility: The Bake function is suitable for a wide variety of recipes, including but not limited to:

o Breads and rolls

o Cakes and cupcakes

o Cookies and brownies

o Pizzas and calzones

o Casseroles and baked pasta dishes

o Roasts and baked meats

o Vegetables and side dishes

✓ Customization: You can customize the cooking time and temperature based on your specific recipe, ensuring that your baked goods turn out just the way you want them. This adaptability is especially important for achieving the perfect texture and doneness.

✓ Precision Baking: The Bake function provides a controlled environment, allowing you to bake delicate pastries to perfection, achieving the ideal rise, color, and texture for your baked goods.

✓ Hands-On Baking: While the Ninja Foodi Possible Cooker Pro takes care of maintaining the temperature and even heat distribution, you'll still be involved in the baking process, including preparing and placing the items in the cooking chamber and checking for doneness.

✓ Time-Saving: Baking in this appliance can often be faster than conventional ovens due to its compact size and efficient heating elements.

✓ Energy Efficiency: Baking in the Ninja Foodi Possible Cooker Pro is energy-efficient, as it heats up quickly and maintains consistent temperatures, potentially reducing overall energy consumption compared to larger ovens.

6. THE SAUTE/SEAR FUNCTION

The "Saute/Sear" function on the Ninja Foodi Possible Cooker Pro is a versatile cooking option designed to brown and sear ingredients quickly, allowing you to build flavor in various dishes.

How it works:

✓ High Heat: The Saute/Sear function generates high heat, typically reaching temperatures around **350°F to 400°F (177°C to 204°C)**. This high temperature is perfect for quickly browning and caramelizing the surfaces of ingredients, such as meats, vegetables, and aromatics.

✓ Preheating: Before you begin sauteing or searing, the appliance will preheat to the desired temperature. It's important to wait until it reaches the set temperature to ensure even and efficient cooking.

✓ Searing: Searing is a crucial step in many recipes, especially those involving meats like steaks, pork chops, or chicken breasts. It creates a flavorful crust on the exterior of the meat, sealing in juices and enhancing the overall taste.

✓ Sauteing: The Saute/Sear function is also excellent for sauteing vegetables, mushrooms, onions, garlic, or any ingredients that benefit from quick cooking in a hot pan. Sauteing at high heat helps develop rich flavors and textures.

✓ One-Pot Cooking: The Ninja Foodi Possible Cooker Pro's Saute/Sear function often allows you to saute or sear ingredients in the same pot or cooking chamber where you'll be preparing the rest of your dish. This minimizes cleanup and maximizes flavor by incorporating the browned bits from the sauteing or searing process into your recipe.

✓ Customization: You have control over the cooking time and can adjust it according to your specific recipe requirements. This adaptability ensures that you achieve the desired level of browning and doneness.

✓ Deglazing: After sauteing or searing, you can deglaze the pan by adding liquid (e.g., broth, wine, or sauce) to the hot cooking chamber. This helps release the flavorful browned bits from the bottom of the pan and incorporates them into your dish for added depth of flavor.

✓ Enhanced Flavor: The Maillard reaction, which occurs during searing, caramelizes sugars and proteins, creating complex and savory flavors in your dishes.

✓ Quick and Efficient: The Saute/Sear function allows you to achieve the browning and searing process much faster than traditional stovetop methods.

✓ Versatility: This function is not limited to meats and vegetables; you can also use it for stir-frying, browning ground meats, or quickly sauteing spices and herbs before incorporating them into your recipes.

7. THE SOUS VIDE FUNCTION

The Sous Vide function on the Ninja Foodi Possible Cooker Pro allows you to perform sous vide cooking, a precision cooking technique that involves cooking vacuum-sealed food in a water bath at a controlled and consistent temperature.

How it works:

✓ Temperature Precision: The key feature of sous vide cooking is precise temperature control. The Ninja Foodi Possible Cooker Pro maintains a steady water temperature within a fraction of a degree of your desired cooking temperature, typically in the range of **100°F to 195°F (37°C to 90°C)**. This precision ensures that your food cooks evenly and to the exact doneness you desire.

✓ Vacuum Sealing: Before cooking, you'll need to vacuum-seal your food in a food-grade plastic bag or pouch. This airtight seal prevents water from entering the bag and preserves the food's natural flavors and juices.

✓ Cooking Time: Sous vide cooking often involves longer cooking times, which can range from 30 minutes to several hours or even days, depending on the type of food and its thickness. Longer cooking times are common for tougher cuts of meat that require tenderization.

✓ Consistent Results: Because the temperature remains constant throughout the cooking process, sous vide cooking yields consistent and predictable results every time. Your food will reach the exact level of doneness you desire, whether it's medium-rare steak, perfectly cooked chicken breast, or a custard with a silky texture.

✓ Tenderizing: Sous vide is exceptional at tenderizing tough cuts of meat. The prolonged, low-temperature cooking process breaks down collagen and connective tissues, resulting in meat that is incredibly tender while maintaining its natural juices.

✓ Minimal Supervision: Once you've set the temperature and placed the sealed food in the water bath, you can largely leave it unattended. This makes it a convenient cooking method, especially for busy individuals.

✓ Finishing Steps: After sous vide cooking, some recipes may call for finishing steps, such as searing meat in a hot pan or grilling it briefly to develop a flavorful crust on the outside. This step enhances the overall texture and appearance of the dish.

✓ Wide Range of Foods: Sous vide is versatile and can be used to cook a variety of foods, including proteins like steak, chicken, fish, and eggs, as well as vegetables, fruits, and desserts.

✓ Safety: The precise temperature control of sous vide cooking ensures that food is pasteurized and safe to eat without overcooking it.

8. THE STEAM FUNCTION

✓ The "Steam" function on the Ninja Foodi Possible Cooker Pro is a versatile cooking method that uses hot steam to cook food. Here's an explanation of how this function works:

✓ Steam Generation: The Steam function produces a continuous flow of hot steam within the cooking chamber, typically at a temperature between **200°F to 212°F (93°C to 100°C)**. This steam surrounds and envelops the food, gently cooking it by transferring heat through condensation.

✓ Healthy Cooking: Steam cooking is considered a healthy cooking method because it doesn't require the addition of oil or fats. It helps retain the natural flavors, colors, and nutrients in your food.

✓ Fast and Efficient: Steam cooking is known for its speed and efficiency. The hot steam quickly penetrates the food, reducing cooking times compared to other methods like boiling or baking.

✓ Versatility: The Steam function is versatile and suitable for a wide range of foods, including vegetables, seafood, poultry, dumplings, rice, and more. It's especially effective for cooking foods that are easily overcooked or require precise doneness, such as delicate fish fillets or tender vegetables.

✓ Retained Nutrients: Because steam cooking involves minimal heat exposure and doesn't require submersion in water, it preserves the vitamins, minerals, and natural flavors of your ingredients better than some other cooking methods.

✓ Customizable: Depending on your recipe, you can customize the cooking time and temperature to achieve the desired results. Different foods may require different steam settings for optimal cooking.

✓ Even Cooking: Steam evenly surrounds the food, ensuring that it cooks uniformly. There are no hot spots or direct contact with a heating element, reducing the risk of overcooking or burning.

✓ Moisture Retention: Steam cooking helps retain moisture in your food, making it a great choice for items like steamed buns, dumplings, and moist, succulent meats.

✓ Easy Cleanup: Since steam cooking doesn't involve oil or direct contact with heating elements, it typically results in minimal mess, making cleanup a breeze.

✓ Stacking and Layering: Some steam cooking setups allow you to stack or layer different ingredients, enabling you to prepare a complete meal all at once, with different components cooked to perfection.

Setting up the Ninja Foodi Possible Cooker pro

Setting up your Ninja Foodi Possible Cooker Pro is a straightforward process. Follow these steps to get started:

Step 1: Unbox and Inspect

Carefully unpack the appliance and remove all packaging materials. Ensure that all included accessories and components are present.

Step 2: Read the User Manual

Before proceeding, read the user manual that comes with the appliance. It contains important safety information, usage guidelines, and maintenance instructions.

Step 3: Set up the Appliance

Choose a suitable location for your Ninja Foodi Possible Cooker Pro. Ensure it is on a flat, stable, and heat-resistant surface.

Leave enough space around the appliance for proper ventilation and safe operation.

Step 4: Power Connection

Plug the appliance into a standard electrical outlet with the correct voltage. Make sure the outlet is grounded.

Step 5: Initial Cleaning

Before using the appliance for the first time, clean all removable parts, such as the cooking pot, cooking rack, and any accessories. You can typically wash these parts with warm, soapy water.

Step 6: Familiarize Yourself with Controls

Take a moment to understand the control panel and buttons on the appliance. Familiarize yourself with the various cooking functions and settings.

Step 7: Lid Placement

Ensure that the appliance's lid is properly placed and locked in position before use. Follow the instructions in the user manual to ensure correct placement.

Step 8: Preheat (Optional)

Depending on the cooking function you intend to use, you may need to preheat the appliance. Refer to your specific recipe instructions for guidance on whether preheating is necessary.

Step 9: Select a Cooking Function

Use the control panel to select the desired cooking function. The Ninja Foodi Possible Cooker Pro offers multiple cooking options, such as slow cook, braise, keep warm, proof, bake, saute/sear, sous vide, and steam.

Step 10: Adjust Settings

Depending on the cooking function, you may need to adjust settings such as time and temperature to match your recipe's requirements. Use the control panel to make these adjustments.

Step 11: Cooking Process

Once you've selected the cooking function and adjusted settings, follow your recipe instructions to prepare and place the ingredients in the appliance. Make sure the lid is properly closed.

General cooking tips for the Ninja Foodi Possible Cooker Pro

Here are some general cooking tips to help you make the most of your Ninja Foodi Possible Cooker Pro:

- Read the User Manual: Start by thoroughly reading the user manual that comes with your appliance. It contains valuable information about safety guidelines, usage instructions, and maintenance tips specific to your model.

- Preheat When Necessary: Some cooking functions may require preheating, while others do not. Always check your recipe instructions to determine if preheating is necessary for the best results.

- Use the Right Accessories: Ensure you're using the appropriate accessories and cooking racks for your specific recipe. The Ninja Foodi Possible Cooker Pro often comes with a variety of accessories like a cooking pot, rack, and air frying basket. Choose the ones that suit your cooking needs.

- Layer Ingredients Carefully: When stacking or layering ingredients in the cooking pot or basket, be mindful of how they cook. Place items that need longer cooking times at the bottom and those that cook quickly at the top.

- Avoid Overcrowding: While the appliance is spacious, avoid overcrowding the cooking chamber, as it can affect airflow and cooking results. It's often better to cook in batches if necessary.

- Use Cooking Liquid: For certain cooking functions like slow cooking, braising, or steaming, using a flavorful liquid (e.g., broth, wine, sauce) can enhance the final taste of your dishes. Be sure not to overfill the cooking pot.

- Monitor Cooking Progress: Keep an eye on your cooking progress, especially when trying a new recipe. The Ninja Foodi Possible Cooker Pro usually provides a timer and notifications, but it's essential to ensure your food isn't overcooking or burning.

- Temperature and Time Adjustments: Get comfortable with adjusting cooking temperatures and times based on your preferences and specific recipes. Experimentation will help you achieve your desired results.

- Safety First: Always use oven mitts or heat-resistant gloves when handling hot components. Be cautious when opening the lid, as hot steam may escape.

- Experiment and Have Fun: The Ninja Foodi Possible Cooker Pro is a versatile appliance. Don't be afraid to experiment with different recipes and cooking functions. It's a great way to discover new flavors and dishes.

- Maintenance and Cleaning: After each use, clean the removable parts and the cooking chamber according to the user manual's instructions. Regular maintenance ensures longevity and optimal performance.

- Ventilation: Ensure that the appliance is placed in an area with adequate ventilation to allow hot air to dissipate. Avoid placing it under cabinets or in confined spaces.

- Safety Precautions: Always follow safety guidelines and precautions outlined in the user manual, such as electrical safety, proper handling of hot components, and safe cleaning practices.

- Keep Recipes Handy: Keep your favorite recipes and cooking times on hand for quick reference, especially if you frequently cook the same dishes.

Maintenance and cleaning guidelines

Proper maintenance and cleaning are essential to keep your Ninja Foodi Possible Cooker Pro functioning optimally and ensure safe and hygienic cooking. Here are some maintenance and cleaning guidelines:

Before Cleaning:

Unplug the Appliance: Before you start cleaning, ensure that the appliance is unplugged and completely cooled down.

Remove Accessories: Take out any removable parts, such as the cooking pot, cooking rack, air frying basket, and any other accessories that can be removed.

Cleaning the Exterior:

Exterior Surface: Wipe down the exterior of the appliance with a damp cloth or sponge. Use a mild detergent if necessary. Avoid abrasive cleaners that could scratch the surface.

Control Panel: Clean the control panel with a damp cloth, taking care not to let water seep into the controls.

Cleaning the Removable Parts:

Cooking Pot and Accessories: Wash the cooking pot, cooking rack, and any other removable accessories with warm, soapy water. Use a non-abrasive sponge or cloth. Some parts may be dishwasher safe, so check the user manual for guidance.

Air Frying Basket: If your appliance has an air frying basket, clean it thoroughly, removing any food residue or grease. You may need to use a brush or scrubbing pad to clean the basket's mesh.

Steamer and Drip Tray: If your appliance has a steaming tray or drip tray, clean them as per the user manual's instructions.

Cleaning the Cooking Chamber:

Interior Surface: Wipe down the interior of the cooking chamber with a damp cloth or sponge. For stubborn stains or food residue, use a non-abrasive kitchen cleaner.

Heating Element: Be cautious when cleaning around the heating element, and do not use abrasive materials that may damage it.

Cleaning the Lid:

Lid Components: Check your user manual for instructions on cleaning the lid components. Some models have removable parts that can be washed separately.

Descaling (if applicable):

Water Reservoir: If your appliance has a water reservoir for functions like steam or sous vide, it may require occasional descaling to remove mineral deposits. Follow the manufacturer's descaling instructions in the user manual.

Maintenance Tips

Regular Maintenance: Perform regular maintenance to keep your appliance in good working condition. This includes checking for loose or damaged parts and ensuring that all components are properly seated.

Replace Worn Parts: If any components, such as gaskets or seals, become worn or damaged, replace them promptly to maintain a proper seal and prevent steam or heat loss.

Ventilation: Ensure that the appliance's ventilation areas are free from obstructions to allow proper air circulation and cooling during operation.

Storage: When not in use, store your Ninja Foodi Possible Cooker Pro in a cool, dry place. Make sure it's free from moisture and protected from extreme temperatures.

Safety precautions

✓ Use on a Stable Surface: Place the appliance on a flat, stable, and heat-resistant surface. Avoid setting it on uneven or wobbly surfaces that could cause it to tip over.

✓ Keep Away from Water: Keep the appliance, including the cord and plug, away from water or any liquid. Do not immerse the appliance in water or allow water to enter the electrical components.

✓ Electrical Safety: Plug the appliance into a properly grounded electrical outlet with the correct voltage as indicated in the user manual. Ensure that the electrical cord is in good condition and not damaged.

✓ Avoid Overloading: Do not overfill the cooking pot or cooking chamber, as it can affect cooking results and safety. Follow the recommended maximum capacity guidelines in your user manual.

✓ Prevent Steam Burns: When opening the lid, especially during or after cooking, be cautious of escaping steam, which can cause burns. Open the lid away from your face and body.

✓ Use Oven Mitts or Heat-Resistant Gloves: When handling hot components, including the cooking pot and accessories, always use oven mitts or heat-resistant gloves to protect your hands from burns.

✓ Proper Ventilation: Ensure that the appliance is placed in an area with adequate ventilation to allow hot air to dissipate. Avoid placing it under cabinets or in confined spaces.

✓ Keep Children and Pets Away: Always supervise children and pets when the appliance is in use. The exterior surfaces can become very hot during cooking.

✓ Unplug After Use: After you've finished using the appliance, unplug it from the electrical outlet to prevent accidental activation.

✓ Use Proper Accessories: Only use accessories and replacement parts recommended by the manufacturer. Using unauthorized accessories or parts may pose safety risks.

✓ Properly Close the Lid: Always ensure that the appliance's lid is properly closed and locked in position before cooking. Follow the user manual's instructions for correct lid placement.

✓ Monitor Cooking: While the appliance is in operation, keep an eye on the cooking progress. Ensure that it is functioning correctly and that there are no issues with the cooking process.

✓ Be Cautious with Hot Liquids: When using functions that involve hot liquids, such as steam or sous vide, be careful when handling and pouring to avoid burns.

✓ Avoid Abrasive Cleaners: Use mild detergents and non-abrasive cleaning materials when cleaning the appliance to avoid damaging the surface.

✓ Follow Recipe Guidelines: Always follow recipe instructions, especially when using specific cooking functions, to ensure safe and successful cooking.

✓ Maintenance: Perform regular maintenance, including cleaning and inspection, to keep the appliance in good working condition.

CHAPTER TWO

30-DAY MEAL PLAN

DAY	BREAKFAST	LUNCH	DINNER
1	Steamed Asparagus with Lemon Butter	Chocolate Babka	Lemon Roasted Pork Tenderloin
2	Steamed Jasmine Rice with Coconut Milk	Oatmeal Raisin Cookies	BBQ Beef Brisket
3	Steamed Veggie and Tofu Stir-Fry	Coconut Macaroons	Beef Sloppy Joes
4	Steamed Shrimp with Old Bay Seasoning	Peanut Butter Cookies	Vegetable Beef Roast with Horseradish
5	Steamed Lemon Pudding Cakes	Red Velvet Cake	Herbed Roasted Pork
6	Steamed Thai Green Curry with Tofu	Gingerbread Cookies	Balsamic Roasted Pork
7	Steamed Pumpkin Custard	Vanilla Cupcakes	Mexican-Style Fish Wraps
8	Steamed Lemon and Herb Asparagus	Chocolate Cake	Mexican Pork Roast
9	Steamed Lemon Garlic Shrimp Pasta	Carrot Cake	Country Style Pork Ribs
10	Pita Bread	Cheesecake	Red Wine Braised Pork Ribs
11	Whole Wheat Bread	Raspberry Thumbprint Cookies	BBQ Pork Ribs
12	Cranberry Orange Bread	Pumpkin Bread	Brazilian Pork Stew
13	Challah	Banana Bread	Chicken Black Olive Stew
14	English Muffins	Strawberry Shortcake	Red Wine Chicken and Mushroom Stew
15	Brioche	Lemon Bars	Sweet Glazed Chicken Drumsticks
16	Flatbread	Blueberry Muffins	Green Pea Chicken with Biscuit Topping
17	Hot Cross Buns	Brownies	Sesame Glazed Chicken
18	Steamed Cod with Lemon Butter Sauce	Chocolate Chip Cookies	Apple Bourbon Pork Chops
19	Steamed Clams in White Wine and Garlic	Lemon Butter Garlic Shrimp	Creamy Chicken and Mushroom Pot Pie
20	Steamed Vegetable Medley with Herb Butter	Sautéed Spinach with Garlic	Pork and Corn Soup
21	Steamed Tofu with Ginger Sesame Sauce	Lemon Butter Garlic Shrimp	Brown Sugar Glazed Chicken

22	Steamed Lobster Tails	Lemon Butter Garlic Scallops	Garlicky Butter Roasted Chicken
23	Steamed Lemon Herb Chicken	Vegetarian Stir-Fried Rice	Swiss Cheese Saucy Chicken
24	Steamed Dumplings (Potstickers)	Lemon Butter Garlic Asparagus	Black Bean Mushroom Soup
25	Chive-Topped Smoked Salmon Toast	Cajun Shrimp and Grits	Ham and Sweet Potato Soup
26	Steamed Mussels in White Wine	Thai Red Curry Shrimp	Bouillabaisse Soup
27	Steamed Rice with Vegetables	Creamy Spinach and Artichoke Dip	Portobello Mushroom Soup
28	Steamed Artichokes with Lemon Garlic Aioli	Coq au Vin	Creamy Tortellini Soup
29	Steamed Broccoli with Garlic Butter	Braised Sweet Potatoes with Maple Glaze	Orange Salmon Soup
30	Steamed Salmon with Dill Sauce	Braised Green Beans with Tomatoes	Chunky Pumpkin and Kale Soup

CHAPTER THREE

SLOW COOK RECIPES

Chunky Pumpkin and Kale Soup

Prep Time: 6 1/2 hours
Cooking Time: 6 hours
Servings: 6
Ingredients:
1 sweet onion, chopped
1 red bell pepper, cored and diced
1/2 red chili, chopped
2 tablespoons of olive oil
2 cups pumpkin cubes
2 cups vegetable stock
2 cups water
1 bunch kale, shredded
1/2 teaspoon of cumin seeds
Salt and pepper to taste

Directions:
Put the onion, bell pepper, chili and olive oil in your Ninja Foodi possible cooker pro.
Add the rest of the ingredients and sprinkle with salt and pepper to taste, then mix the ingredients in the cooker until well-combine.
Set the possible cooker settings to "slow cook", then cook at 88ºC (LOW settings) for 6 hours.
Serve the soup warm or chilled.
NUTRITION Calories: 177 | Fat: 9g | Carbs: 24g | Protein: 4g

Orange Salmon Soup

Prep Time: 2 1/4 hours
Cooking Time: 2 hours
Servings: 8
Ingredients:
1 sweet onion, chopped
1 garlic clove, chopped
1 celery stalk, sliced
1 small fennel bulb, sliced
1 cup diced tomatoes
3 salmon fillets, cubed
2 cups vegetable stock
3 cups water
1 lemon, juiced
1 orange, juiced
1/2 teaspoon of grated orange zest
Salt and pepper to taste

Directions:
Mix the onion, garlic, celery, fennel bulb, tomatoes, salmon, stock and water in your Ninja Foodi possible cooker pro.
Stir in the rest of the ingredients and sprinkle with salt and pepper to taste.
Set the possible cooker settings to "slow cook", then cook at 149ºC (HIGH settings) for 2 hours.
Serve the soup warm or chilled.
NUTRITION Calories: 193 | Fat: 6g | Carbs: 11g | Protein: 24g

Creamy Tortellini Soup

Prep Time: 6 1/4 hours
Cooking Time: 6 hours
Servings: 6
Ingredients:
1 shallot, chopped
1 garlic clove, chopped
1/2 pound mushrooms, sliced
1 can condensed cream of mushroom soup
2 cups chicken stock
1 cup water
1/2 teaspoon of dried oregano
1/2 teaspoon of dried basil
1 cup evaporated milk
7 oz. cheese tortellini
Salt and pepper to taste

Directions:
Place the shallot, garlic, mushrooms, cream of mushroom soup, stock, water, dried herbs and milk in your Ninja Foodi possible cooker pro and mix properly.
Add the cheese tortellini and sprinkle with salt and pepper to taste.
Set the possible cooker settings to "slow cook", then cook at 88ºC (LOW settings) for 6 hours.
Serve the soup warm.
NUTRITION Calories: 263 | Fat: 13g | Carbs: 27g | Protein: 10g

Portobello Mushroom Soup

Prep Time: 6 1/4 hours
Cooking Time: 6 hours
Servings: 6
Ingredients:
4 Portobello mushrooms, sliced
1 shallot, chopped
2 garlic cloves, chopped
1 cup diced tomatoes
1 tablespoon tomato paste
2 cups chicken stock
1 can condensed cream of mushroom soup
Salt and pepper to taste
1/2 teaspoon of cumin seeds
1 tablespoon chopped parsley
1 tablespoon chopped cilantro

Directions:
Place the mushrooms, shallot, garlic, tomatoes, tomato paste, stock and mushroom soup in your Ninja Foodi possible cooker pro and mix properly.
Stir in the cumin seeds then sprinkle with salt and pepper to taste.
Set the possible cooker settings to "slow cook", then cook at 88ºC (LOW settings) for 6 hours.
When done, add the chopped parsley and cilantro.
Serve the soup warm.

NUTRITION Calories: 134 | Fat: 5g | Carbs: 19g | Protein: 6g

Bouillabaisse Soup

Prep Time: 6 1/2 hours
Cooking Time: 6 hours
Servings: 8
Ingredients:
1 shallot, chopped
2 garlic cloves, chopped
1 red bell pepper, cored and diced
1 carrot, diced
1 fennel bulb, sliced
1 cup diced tomatoes
2 cups vegetable stock
2 large potatoes, peeled and cubed
1 celery stalk, sliced
1/2 lemon, juiced
1 pound haddock fillets, cubed
Salt and pepper to taste
1 tablespoon chopped parsley

Directions:

Place the shallot, garlic, bell pepper, carrot, fennel, tomatoes and stock in your Ninja Foodi possible cooker pro and mix properly.
Stir in the potatoes, celery, lemon juice, salt and pepper.
Set the possible cooker settings to "slow cook", then cook at 149ºC (HIGH settings) for 1 hour.
Add the haddock fillets and continue cooking for 5 minutes at 88ºC (LOW settings).
Serve the soup warm, topped with chopped parsley

NUTRITION Calories: 142 | Fat: 1g | Carbs: 28 | Protein: 8g

Ham and Sweet Potato Soup

Prep Time: 3 1/2 hours
Cooking Time: 3 hours
Servings: 6
Ingredients:
1 1/2 cups diced ham
1 sweet onion, chopped
1 carrot, diced
1 celery stalk, diced
1 parsnip, diced
2 large sweet potatoes, peeled and cubed
2 cups chicken stock
2 cups water
1 bay leaf
1 thyme sprig
Salt and pepper to taste

Directions:
Place all the necessary ingredients in your Ninja Foodi possible cooker pro and mix properly.
Add salt and pepper to taste
Set the possible cooker settings to "slow cook", then cook at 149ºC (HIGH settings) for 3 hours.
Serve the soup warm and fresh.

NUTRITION Calories: 176 | Fat: 2g | Carbs: 8g | Protein: 8g

Black Bean Mushroom Soup

Prep Time: 6 1/2 hours
Cooking Time: 6 hours
Servings: 8
Ingredients:
1 shallot, chopped
2 garlic cloves, chopped
1 can (15 oz.) black beans, drained
1/2 pound mushrooms, sliced
1 can fire roasted tomatoes
2 cups vegetable stock
4 cups water
1/2 teaspoon of mustard seeds
1/2 teaspoon of cumin seeds
Salt and pepper to taste
2 tablespoons of chopped parsley

Directions:
Place the shallot, garlic and black beans with the mushrooms, tomatoes, stock, water and seeds in your Ninja Foodi possible cooker pro and mix properly.
Add salt and pepper to taste
Set the possible cooker settings to "slow cook", then cook at 88oC (LOW settings) for 6 hours.
When done, add the parsley and serve the soup warm.
NUTRITION Calories: 117 | **Fat:** 1g | **Carbs:** 21g | **Protein:** 7g

Garlicky Butter Roasted Chicke

Prep Time: 8 1/4 hours
Cooking Time: 8 hours
Servings: 8
Ingredients:
1 whole chicken
1/4 cup butter, softened
6 garlic cloves, minced
2 tablespoons of chopped parsley
1 teaspoon of dried sage
Salt and pepper to taste
1/2 cup chicken stock

Directions:
Combine the butter, garlic, parsley, sage, salt and pepper in your Ninja Foodi possible cooker pro.
Put the chicken on your chopping board and carefully lift up the skin on its breast and thighs, then pour the butter mixture in the space.
Put the chicken in your Ninja Foodi possible cooker pro, then add the stock.
Set the possible cooker settings to "slow cook", then cook at 88oC (LOW settings) for 8 hours.
Serve the chicken fresh with your favorite side dish.
NUTRITION Calories: 371 | **Fat:** 26g | **Carbs:** 1g | **Protein:** 30g

Swiss Cheese Saucy Chicken

Prep Time: 3 1/4 hours
Cooking Time: 3 hours
Servings: 4
Ingredients:
4 boneless chicken breasts
1 celery stalk, sliced
1 shallot, sliced
Salt and pepper to taste
1 can cream of mushrooms soup
1/2 cup chicken stock
1 cup grated Swiss cheese

Directions:
Season the chicken with salt and pepper up to your taste.
Put the chicken in your Ninja Foodi possible cooker pro and add the remaining ingredients.
Set the possible cooker settings to "slow cook", then cook at 149oC (HIGH settings) for 3 hours.
Serve the chicken warm with your favorite side dish.
NUTRITION Calories: 423 | **Fat:** 22g | **Carbs:** 7g | **Protein:** 48g

Brown Sugar Glazed Chicken

Prep Time: 6 1/4 hours
Cooking Time: 6 hours
Servings: 4
Ingredients:
4 chicken thighs
2 tablespoons of brown sugar
1 teaspoon of cumin powder
1/2 teaspoon of chili powder
1/2 teaspoon of garlic powder
2 tablespoons of balsamic vinegar
1 tablespoon soy sauce
1/2 cup chicken stock

Directions:
Combine the brown sugar, cumin powder, chili, balsamic vinegar and soy sauce in a bowl.
Brush the chicken with the mixture and rub it well into the skin.
Put the chicken in your Ninja Foodi possible cooker pro, then add the stock in the pot
Set the possible cooker settings to "slow cook", then cook at 88oC (LOW settings) for 6 hours.
Serve the chicken warm.
NUTRITION Calories: 308 | **Fat:** 18g | **Carbs:** 10g | **Protein:** 25g

Pork and Corn Soup

Prep Time: 8 1/4 hours
Cooking Time: 8 hours
Servings: 8
Ingredients:
1 pound pork roast, cubed
1 sweet onion, chopped
2 bacon slices, chopped
1 garlic clove, chopped
2 carrots, sliced
1 celery stalk, sliced
2 yellow bell peppers, cored and diced
2 cups frozen sweet corn
1/2 teaspoon of cumin seeds
1/2 red chili, sliced
2 cups chicken stock
4 cups water
Salt and pepper to taste
2 tablespoons of chopped cilantro

Directions:
Place the pork roast, sweet onion, bacon and garlic in a skillet and cook for 5 mins, stirring throughout.
Transfer the mixture in your Ninja Foodi possible cooker pro and add the carrots, celery, bell peppers, sweet corn, cumin seeds, red chili, stock, water, salt and pepper.
Set the possible cooker settings to "slow cook", then cook at 88°C (LOW settings) for 8 hours.
When done, add the chopped cilantro and serve the soup warm.

NUTRITION Calories: 227 | Fat: 10g | Carbs: 21g | Protein: 14g

Creamy Chicken and Mushroom Pot Pie

Prep Time: 6 1/4 hours
Cooking Time: 6 hours
Servings: 6
Ingredients:
4 cups sliced cremini mushrooms
4 carrots, sliced
2 chicken breasts, cubed
1 large onion, chopped
1 cup frozen peas
1 cup vegetable stock
Salt and pepper to taste
1/2 teaspoon of dried thyme
1 sheet puff pastry

Directions:
Place the mushrooms, carrots, chicken, onion, peas, stock and thyme in your Ninja Foodi possible cooker pro and mix properly.
Season with salt and pepper to taste then top with the puff pastry.
Set the possible cooker settings to "slow cook", then cook at 88°C (LOW settings) for 6 hours.
Serve the pot pie warm and fresh.

NUTRITION Calories: 363 | Fat: 18g | Carbs: 25g | Protein: 24g

Apple Bourbon Pork Chops

Prep Time: 8 1/4 hours
Cooking Time: 8 hours
Servings: 6
Ingredients:
6 pork chops
4 red apples, cored and sliced
1/2 cup applesauce
1/4 cup bourbon
1/2 cup chicken stock
1 thyme sprig
1 rosemary sprig
Salt and pepper to taste

Directions:
Sprinkle the pork chops with salt and pepper.
Combine the apples, applesauce, bourbon, stock, thyme and rosemary in your Ninja Foodi possible cooker pro.
Put the pork chops on top; set the possible cooker settings to "slow cook", then cook at 88°C (LOW settings) for 8 hours.
Serve the pork chops with the sauce found in the pot.

NUTRITION Calories: 335 | Fat: 14g | Carbs: 20g | Protein: 28g

Sesame Glazed Chicken

Prep Time: 3 1/4 hours
Cooking Time: 3 hours
Servings: 6
Ingredients:
6 chicken thighs
1 tablespoon sesame oil
2 tablespoon soy sauce
1 tablespoon brown sugar
2 tablespoons of fresh orange juice
2 tablespoons of hoisin sauce
1 teaspoon of grated ginger
1 tablespoon cornstarch
2 tablespoons of water
1 tablespoon sesame seeds
Directions:
Place all the necessary ingredients in your Ninja Foodi possible cooker pro.
Set the possible cooker settings to "slow cook", then cook at 149°C (HIGH settings) for 3 hours.
Serve the chicken warm with your favorite side dish.
NUTRITION Calories: 324 | Fat: 19g | Carbs: 9g | Protein: 27g

Green Pea Chicken with Biscuit Topping

Prep Time: 6 1/2 hours
Cooking Time: 6 hours
Servings: 6
Ingredients:
1 shallot, chopped
1 leek, sliced
2 garlic cloves, chopped
2 chicken breasts, cubed
1 1/2 cups green peas
1/2 pound baby carrots
1 tablespoon cornstarch
1 cup vegetables tock
1/4 cup white wine
1 cup all-purpose flour
1/2 cup butter, chilled and cubed
1/2 cup buttermilk, chilled
Salt and pepper to taste
Directions:
Place the shallot, leek, garlic, chicken, green peas, baby carrots, cornstarch, stock and wine in your Ninja Foodi possible cooker pro and mix properly.
Sprinkle with salt and pepper to taste.
For the topping, blend the flour, butter, buttermilk, salt and pepper in your blender.
Pour the mixture over the vegetables in the Ninja Foodi possible cooker pro.
Set the possible cooker settings to "slow cook", then cook at 88°C (LOW settings) for 6 hours. Serve the dish warm.

NUTRITION Calories: 477 | Fat: 23g | Carbs: 45g | Protein: 22g

Sweet Glazed Chicken Drumsticks

Prep Time: 5 1/4 hours
Cooking Time: 5 hours
Servings: 4
Ingredients:
2 pounds chicken drumsticks
1 teaspoon of grated ginger
1 cup pineapple juice
2 tablespoons of soy sauce
2 tablespoons of brown sugar
1/4 teaspoon of chili powder
2 green onions, chopped
1/4 cup chicken stock
White rice for serving
Directions:
Place the drumsticks, ginger, pineapple juice, soy sauce, brown sugar, chili, stock and green onions in your Ninja Foodi possible cooker pro and mix properly.
Add salt and pepper to taste, then set the possible cooker settings to "slow cook" and cook at 88°C (LOW settings) for 5 hours.
Serve the dish warm, over cooked white rice.
NUTRITION Calories: 387 | Fat: 14g | Carbs: 28g | Protein: 37g

Red Wine Chicken and Mushroom Stew

Prep Time: 6 1/2 hours
Cooking Time: 6 hours
Servings: 6
Ingredients:
6 chicken thighs
1 large onion, chopped
4 garlic cloves, minced
4 cups sliced mushrooms
1/2 cup red wine
1 cup chicken stock
1 bay leaf
1 thyme sprig
Salt and pepper to taste
Directions:
Combine the chicken, onion, garlic, mushrooms, red wine, stock, bay leaf and thyme in your Ninja Foodi possible cooker pro.
Season with salt and pepper to taste
Set the possible cooker settings to "slow cook", then cook at 88°C (LOW settings) for 6 hours. Serve the stew warm and fresh.
NUTRITION Calories: 361 | Fat: 20g | Carbs: 7g | Protein: 30g

Chicken Black Olive Stew

Prep Time: 6 1/4 hours
Cooking Time: 6 hours
Servings: 6
Ingredients:
6 chicken thighs
2 tablespoons of olive oil
4 garlic cloves, minced
1 shallot, chopped
1/4 cup dry white wine
2 tablespoons of tomato paste
1/2 cup tomato sauce
1/4 teaspoon of chili powder
1 can (28 oz.) diced tomatoes
1/2 cup pitted black olives
1/2 cup pitted Kalamata olives
Salt and pepper to taste
Directions:
Combine all the necessary ingredients in your Ninja Foodi possible cooker pro, then add salt and pepper to taste.
Set the possible cooker settings to "slow cook", then cook at 88ºC (LOW settings) for 6 hours.
The dish is best served warm.
NUTRITION Calories: 377 | Fat: 21g | Carbs: 13g | Protein: 31g

Brazilian Pork Stew

Prep Time: 7 1/4 hours
Cooking Time: 7 hours
Servings: 6
Ingredients:
1/2 pound dried black beans
1 1/2 pounds pork shoulder, cubed
2 sweet onions, chopped
4 bacon slices, chopped
4 garlic cloves, chopped
1 teaspoon of cumin seeds
1/2 teaspoon of ground coriander
2 bay leaves
1 teaspoon of white wine vinegar
2 cups chicken stock
Salt and pepper to taste

Directions:
Combine the beans and pork with the remaining ingredients in your Ninja Foodi possible cooker pro.
Add salt and pepper to taste.
Set the possible cooker settings to "slow cook", then cook at 88ºC (LOW settings) for 7 hours.
Serve the stew warm and fresh.
NUTRITION Calories: 418 | Fat: 15g | Carbs: 40g | Protein: 29g

BBQ Pork Ribs

Prep Time: 11 1/4 hours
Cooking Time: 11 hours
Servings: 8
Ingredients:
5 pounds pork short ribs
2 cups BBQ sauce
1 large onion, sliced
1 celery stalk, sliced
1 tablespoon Dijon mustard
1 teaspoon of chili powder
1 tablespoon brown sugar
4 garlic cloves, minced
1/4 cup chicken stock
Salt and pepper to taste

Directions:
Combine the pork short ribs, BBQ sauce, onion, celery and mustard, and also chili, sugar, garlic and stock in your Ninja Foodi possible cooker pro.
Add salt and pepper to taste
Set the possible cooker settings to "slow cook", then cook at 88ºC (LOW settings) for 11 hours.
Serve the pork ribs warm and fresh.
NUTRITION Calories: 691 | Fat: 46g | Carbs: 28g | Protein: 41g

Red Wine Braised Pork Ribs

Prep Time: 8 1/4 hours
Cooking Time: 8 hours
Servings: 8
Ingredients:
5 pounds pork short ribs
4 tablespoons of brown sugar
1 tablespoon molasses
2 tablespoons of olive oil
1 teaspoon of chili powder
1 teaspoon of cumin powder
1 teaspoon of dried thyme
1 teaspoon of salt
1 cup BBQ sauce
1 cup red wine

Directions:
Combine the brown sugar, molasses, olive oil, chili powder, cumin powder, thyme and salt in a bowl.
Pour the mixture over the pork ribs and rub the meat well with the spice. Put in your Ninja Foodi possible cooker pro.
Add the BBQ sauce and red wine; Set the possible cooker settings to "slow cook", then cook at 88ºC (LOW settings) for 8 hours.
Serve the pork ribs warm.
NUTRITION Calories: 659 | Fat: 46g | Carbs: 21g | Protein: 31g

Fennel Infused Pork Ham

Prep Time: 6 1/4 hours
Cooking Time: 6 hours
Servings: 8
Ingredients:
4-5 pounds piece of pork ham
2 fennel bulbs, sliced
1 orange, zested and juiced
1/2 cup white wine
1 cup chicken stock
2 bay leaves
1 thyme sprig
Salt and pepper to taste

Directions:
Combine the fennel, orange zest, orange juice, white wine, chicken stock, bay leaves and thyme in your Ninja Foodi possible cooker pro.
Season with salt and pepper and place the ham on top.
Set the possible cooker settings to "slow cook", then cook at 88°C (LOW settings) for 6 hours.
Slice and serve the ham warm.

NUTRITION Calories: 374 | **Fat:** 18g | **Carbs:** 7g | **Protein:** 45g

Country Style Pork Ribs

Prep Time: 6 1/4 hours
Cooking Time: 6 hours
Servings: 4
Ingredients:
3 pounds short pork ribs
1 teaspoon of salt
1 teaspoon of garlic powder
1 tablespoon brown sugar
1 teaspoon of dried thyme
1 cup pineapple juice

Directions:
Season the pork ribs with salt, garlic powder, brown sugar and thyme and place in your Ninja Foodi possible cooker pro.
Add the pineapple juice; Set the possible cooker settings to "slow cook", then cook at 88°C (LOW settings) for 6 hours.
Serve the pork ribs warm and fresh.

NUTRITION Calories: 545 | **Fat:** 36g | **Carbs:** 11g | **Protein:** 42g

Mexican Pork Roast

Prep Time: 8 1/4 hours
Cooking Time: 8 hours
Servings: 6
Ingredients:
2 pounds pork shoulder, cubed
1 can fire roasted tomatoes
2 carrots, sliced
2 celery stalks, sliced
1 large onion, chopped
1 teaspoon of smoked paprika
1/2 teaspoon of cumin powder
1 bay leaf
1 cup chicken stock
Salt and pepper to taste

Directions:
Combine the pork shoulder, tomatoes, carrots, celery, onion, paprika, cumin powder, bay leaf, stock, salt and pepper.
Set the possible cooker settings to "slow cook", then cook at 88°C (LOW settings) for 8 hours.
Serve the pork roast warm and fresh.

NUTRITION Calories: 355 | **Fat:** 18g | **Carbs:** 17g | **Protein:** 30g

Balsamic Roasted Pork

Prep Time: 6 1/4 hours
Cooking Time: 6 hours
Servings: 8
Ingredients:
4 pounds pork shoulder, cubed
2 tablespoons of brown sugar
1 teaspoon of five-spice powder
1 teaspoon of garlic powder
2 tablespoons of honey
1 teaspoon of hot sauce
1/4 cup balsamic vinegar
Salt and pepper to taste

Directions:
Combine the sugar, five-spice powder, honey and hot sauce in a bowl. Pour the mixture over the pork and rub it properly.
Put the pork in your Ninja Foodi possible cooker pro and add the vinegar.
Season with salt and pepper
Set the possible cooker settings to "slow cook", then cook at 88°C (LOW settings) for 6 hours.
Serve the pork warm and fresh with your favorite side dish.

NUTRITION Calories: 356 | **Fat:** 18g | **Carbs:** 11g | **Protein:** 33g

Herbed Roasted Pork

Prep Time: 6 1/4 hours
Cooking Time: 6 hours
Servings: 6
Ingredients:
2 pounds pork tenderloin
1 cup chopped parsley
1/2 cup chopped cilantro
4 basil leaves
1/4 cup pine nuts
1/2 cup chicken stock
1/2 cup grated Parmesan
Salt and pepper to taste
1 lemon, juiced

Directions:
Combine the parsley, cilantro, basil, pine nuts, stock, cheese, lemon juice, salt and pepper in a blender and blend until smooth.
Mix the pork tenderloin with the herbed mixture; Set the possible cooker settings to "slow cook", then cook at 88ºC (LOW settings) for 6 hours.
Serve the pork with your favorite side dish.

NUTRITION Calories: 328 | Fat: 17g | Carbs: 5g | Protein: 37g

Chili BBQ Ribs

Prep Time: 8 1/2 hours
Cooking Time: 8 hours
Servings: 8
Ingredients:
6 pounds pork short ribs
2 cups BBQ sauce
1 1/2 teaspoon of chili powder
1 teaspoon of cumin powder
2 tablespoons of brown sugar
2 tablespoons of red wine vinegar
1 teaspoon of Worcestershire sauce
Salt and pepper to taste

Directions:
Combine the BBQ sauce, chili powder, sugar, vinegar, Worcestershire sauce, salt and pepper in a Ninja Foodi possible cooker pro.
Add the short ribs and mix until well coated.
Set the possible cooker settings to "slow cook", then cook at 88ºC (LOW settings) for 8 1/4 hours.
Serve the ribs warm and fresh.

NUTRITION Calories: 793 | Fat: 54g | Carbs: 34g | Protein: 45g

Lemon Roasted Pork Tenderloin

Prep Time: 7 1/4 hours
Cooking Time: 7 hours
Servings: 6
Ingredients:
2 pounds pork tenderloin
1 lemon, sliced
1 teaspoon of black pepper kernels
1 cup canola oil
1 cup vegetable stock
Salt and pepper to taste

Directions:
Combine all the necessary ingredients in your Ninja Foodi possible cooker pro.
Add salt and pepper to taste
Set the possible cooker settings to "slow cook", then cook at 88ºC (LOW settings) for 7 hours.
Slice the pork and serve it warm.

NUTRITION Calories: 319 | Fat: 21g | Carbs: 4g | Protein: 31g

BBQ Beef Brisket

Prep Time: 6 1/4 hours
Cooking Time: 6 hours
Servings: 8
Ingredients:
4 pounds beef brisket
2 tablespoons of brown sugar
1 teaspoon of cumin powder
1 teaspoon of smoked paprika
1 teaspoon of chili powder
1 teaspoon of celery seeds
1 teaspoon of salt
1/4 cup apple cider vinegar
1/2 cup beef stock
1 cup ketchup
1 tablespoon Worcestershire sauce
2 tablespoons of soy sauce

Directions:
Combine the sugar, cumin powder, paprika, chili powder, celery seeds and salt in a bowl.
Pour the mixture over the beef and rub it well into the meat.
Combine the vinegar, stock, ketchup, Worcestershire sauce and soy sauce in your Ninja Foodi possible cooker pro.
Add the beef; Set the possible cooker settings to "slow cook", then cook at 88ºC (LOW settings) for 6 hours.
Serve the beef brisket sliced and warm.
NUTRITION Calories: 502 | Fat: 31g | Carbs: 19g | Protein: 36g

Beef Sloppy Joes

Prep Time: 7 1/4 hours
Cooking Time: 7 hours
Servings: 8
Ingredients:
2 pounds ground beef
2 large onions, finely chopped
1 tablespoon Worcestershire sauce
1/4 cup hot ketchup
1/2 cup tomato juice
1/2 cup beef stock
Salt and pepper to taste
Bread buns for serving

Directions:
Combine all the necessary ingredients except buns in your Ninja Foodi possible cooker pro.
Add salt and pepper to taste
Set the possible cooker settings to "slow cook", then cook at 88°C (LOW settings) for 7 hours.
When done, serve the dish in bread buns.
NUTRITION Calories: 355 | Fat: 20g | Carbs: 16g | Protein: 27g

Vegetable Beef Roast with Horseradish

Prep Time: 6 1/2 hours
Cooking Time: 6 hours
Servings: 8
Ingredients:
4 pounds beef roast, trimmed of fat
4 large potatoes, peeled and halved
2 large carrots, sliced
2 onions, quartered
2 cups sliced mushrooms
2 cups snap peas
1 celery root, peeled and cubed
1 cup beef stock
1 cup water
Salt and pepper to taste
1/4 cup prepared horseradish for serving

Directions:
Combine all the ingredients except horseradish in your Ninja Foodi possible cooker pro, then season with salt and pepper to taste.
Set the possible cooker settings to "slow cook", then cook at 88°C (LOW settings) for 6 hours.
When done, serve the roast warm with prepared horseradish as sauce.
NUTRITION Calories: 406 | Fat: 9g | Carbs: 48g | Protein: 33g

Cowboy Beef

Prep Time: 6 1/4 hours
Cooking Time: 6 hours
Servings: 6
Ingredients:
2 1/2 pounds beef sirloin roast
6 bacon slices, chopped
2 onions, sliced
4 garlic cloves, chopped
1 can (15 oz.) red beans, drained
1 cup BBQ sauce
1 teaspoon of chili powder
Salt and pepper to taste
Coleslaw for serving

Directions:
Combine the beef sirloin, bacon, onions, garlic, red beans, BBQ sauce, chili powder, salt and pepper in your Ninja Foodi possible cooker pro and cover it.
Set the possible cooker settings to "slow cook", then cook at 88°C (LOW settings) for 6 hours.
Serve the beef warm and fresh, topped with fresh coleslaw.
NUTRITION Calories: 522 | Fat: 23g | Carbs: 34g | Protein: 43g

Sweet and Tangy Short Ribs

Prep Time: 9 1/4 hours
Cooking Time: 9 hours
Servings: 8
Ingredients:
6 pounds beef short ribs
2 cups BBQ sauce
2 red onions, sliced
1/4 cup balsamic vinegar
1/4 cup brown sugar
2 tablespoons of hot sauce
2 tablespoons of apricot preserves
2 tablespoons of Worcestershire sauce
1 tablespoon Dijon mustard
1 teaspoon of garlic powder
1 teaspoon of cumin powder
Salt and pepper to taste

Directions:
Combine the BBQ sauce, onions, vinegar, sugar, apricot preserved, Worcestershire sauce, mustard, garlic powder and cumin powder in your Ninja Foodi possible cooker pro.
Add the short ribs and coat them well.
Set the possible cooker settings to "slow cook", then cook at 88°C (LOW settings) for 9 hours.
Serve the ribs warm.
NUTRITION Calories: 619 | Fat: 28g | Carbs: 47g | Protein: 48g

Beef Stroganoff

Prep Time: 6 1/4 hours
Cooking Time: 6 hours
Servings: 6
Ingredients:
1 1/2 pounds beef stew meat, cubed
1 large onion, chopped
4 garlic cloves, minced
1 tablespoon Worcestershire sauce
1/2 cup water
1 cup cream cheese
Salt and pepper to taste
Cooked pasta for serving

Directions:
Combine all the ingredients except pasta in a Ninja Foodi possible cooker pro.
Add salt and pepper to taste
Set the possible cooker settings to "slow cook", then cook at 88ºC (LOW settings) for 6 hours.
Serve the stroganoff warm and serve it with cooked pasta of your choice.

NUTRITION Calories: 486 | Fat: 32g | Carbs: 6g | Protein: 39g

Corned Beef with Sauerkraut

Prep Time: 8 1/4 hours
Cooking Time: 8 hours
Servings: 6
Ingredients:
3 pounds corned beef brisket
4 large carrot, sliced
1 pound sauerkraut, shredded
1 onion, sliced
1/2 teaspoon of cumin seeds
1 cup beef stock
Salt and pepper to taste

Directions:
Combine all the ingredients in your Ninja Foodi possible cooker pro.
Add salt and pepper to taste
Set the possible cooker settings to "slow cook", then cook at 88ºC (LOW settings) for 8 hours.
Serve the beef sliced and warm, paired with the sauerkraut.

NUTRITION Calories: 575 | Fat: 30g | Carbs: 16g | Protein: 58g

Coffee Beef Roast

Prep Time: 4 1/4 hours
Cooking Time: 4 hours
Servings: 6
Ingredients:
2 pounds beef sirloin
2 tablespoons olive oil
4 garlic cloves, minced
1 cup strong brewed coffee
1/2 cup beef stock
Salt and pepper to taste

Directions:
Combine all the ingredients in your Ninja Foodi possible cooker pro, then add salt and pepper to taste. Cover with a lid and cook on high settings (149ºC) for 4 hours.
Serve the roast warm and fresh with your favorite side dish.

NUTRITION Calories: 344 | Fat: 17g | Carbs: 3g | Protein: 44g

Root Vegetable Beef Stew

Prep Time: 8 1/2 hours
Cooking Time: 8 hours
Servings: 8
Ingredients:
3 pounds beef sirloin roast, cubed
4 carrots, sliced
2 parsnips, sliced
1 celery root, peeled and cubed
4 garlic cloves, chopped
4 large potatoes, peeled and cubed
1 turnip, peeled and cubed
1 bay leaf
1 lemon, juiced
1 teaspoon Worcestershire sauce
1 cup beef stock
Salt and pepper to taste

Directions:
Combine the beef, carrots, parsnips, celery root, garlic, potatoes, turnip, bay leaf, lemon juice, Worcestershire sauce and stock in your Ninja Foodi possible cooker pro.
Add salt and pepper to taste and cover with its lid.
Cook on low settings (88ºC) for 8 hours.
Serve the roast and vegetables warm.

NUTRITION Calories: 44 | Fat: 14g | Carbs: 41g | Protein: 39g

Parmesan Biscuit Pot Pie

Prep Time: 7 1/2 hours
Cooking Time: 7 hours
Servings: 8
Ingredients:
2 tablespoons olive oil
2 garlic cloves, chopped
1 large onion, finely chopped
2 carrots, diced
1 parsnip, diced
1 turnip, diced
2 cups sliced mushrooms
1 cup green peas
Salt and pepper to taste
1/2 cup all-purpose flour
1/2 teaspoon baking powder
1 cup grated Parmesan
1/4 cup butter, chilled and cubed
1/2 cup buttermilk

Directions:
Combine the oil, garlic, onion, carrots, parsnip, turnip, mushrooms, green peas, salt and pepper in your Ninja Foodi possible cooker pro.
Combine the flour, baking powder and Parmesan in your cooker pro.
Combine until sandy then add the buttermilk.
Pour the mixture over the vegetables and cook on low settings (88ºC) for 7 hours.
Serve the pot pie warm or chilled.

NUTRITION Calories: 385 | Fat: 21g | Carbs: 35g | Protein: 12g

Hearty Black Bean Quinoa Chili

Prep Time: 8 1/4 hours
Cooking Time: 8 hours
Servings: 8
Ingredients:
2 cups dried black beans
4 cups vegetable stock
1 can fire roasted tomatoes
2 chipotle peppers, chopped
4 garlic cloves, chopped
1 celery stalk, diced
2 red bell peppers, cored and diced
1/2 teaspoon cumin powder
1/4 cup red quinoa, rinsed
1/4 teaspoon chili powder
Salt and pepper to taste

2 tablespoons chopped parsley for serving

Directions:
Combine the beans, stock, tomatoes, chipotle peppers, garlic, celery, bell peppers, cumin powder, quinoa and chili powder in your Ninja Foodi possible cooker pro.
Add salt and pepper to taste and cook on low settings (88ºC) for 8 hours.
Serve the chili warm, topped with chopped parsley just before serving.

NUTRITION Calories: 231 | Fat: 1g | Carbs: 46g | Protein: 14g

Farro Pumpkin Stew

Prep Time: 6 1/4 hours
Cooking Time: 6 hours
Servings: 6
Ingredients:
2 tablespoons butter
1 cup farro, rinsed
2 cups pumpkin cubes
1 shallot, chopped
1 garlic clove, minced
1/4 teaspoon cumin seeds
1/4 teaspoon fennel seeds
1/4 cup white wine
2 1/2 cups vegetable stock
Salt and pepper to taste
1/2 cup grated Parmesan cheese

Directions:
Mix the butter, faro, pumpkin, shallot, garlic, cumin seeds, fennel seeds, wine and stock in your Ninja Foodi possible cooker pro.
Add salt and pepper to taste and cook on low settings (88ºC) for 6 hours.
Serve the stew warm or chilled.

NUTRITION Calories: 354 | Fat: 10g | Carbs: 54g | Protein: 12g

CHAPTER FOUR

BAKE RECIPES

Chocolate Chip Cookies

Prep Time: 15 minutes
Cook Time: 10 minutes
Servings: About 24 cookies
Ingredients:
2 large eggs
1/2 teaspoon of baking soda
1 teaspoon of salt
1 teaspoon of pure vanilla extract
2 1/4 cups all-purpose flour
1 cup (2 sticks) unsalted butter, softened
1 cup granulated sugar
1 cup packed brown sugar
2 cups semisweet chocolate chips

Directions:
In a clean mixing bowl, beat together the softened butter, granulated sugar, and brown sugar until the mixture becomes light and fluffy.
Introduce the eggs one by one, ensuring thorough blending after each addition. Stir in the vanilla extract.
In another bowl, combine the flour, baking soda, and salt. Gradually incorporate this dry mixture into the wet ingredients, stirring until just blended.
Gently fold in the semisweet chocolate chips.
Using a spoon, drop portions of cookie dough onto a baking sheet lined with parchment paper. Place the sheet inside the Ninja Foodi Possible Cooker Pro and bake at 350°F for approximately 10 minutes or until the edges acquire a golden hue while the center remains slightly soft.
Allow the cookies to cool on a wire rack for a few minutes before serving.
   NUTRITION Calories: 215 | Fat: 10g | Carbs: 30g | Protein: 2.5g

Brownies

Prep Time: 15 minutes
Cook Time: 25-30 minutes
Servings: 16 brownies
Ingredients:
1 teaspoon of vanilla extract
1/4 teaspoon of salt
1 cup all-purpose flour
1 cup unsalted butter
2 cups granulated sugar
4 large eggs
1/2 cup unsweetened cocoa powder

1/2 cup chopped nuts (optional)
Directions:
Preheat your Ninja Foodi possible cooker pro to 350°F.
In a microwave-safe bowl, melt the butter. Stir in the sugar. Beat in the eggs one at a time, then stir in the vanilla. In a separate bowl, combine the cocoa powder, flour, and salt. Gradually add this dry mixture to the wet ingredients, mixing until just combined.
If desired, fold in chopped nuts.
Pour the mixture into a baking dish that has been lightly greased and dusted with flour, ensuring it fits snugly inside your Ninja Foodi Possible Cooker Pro. Position the dish within the cooker pro and allow it to bake for approximately 25-30 minutes, or until a toothpick inserted into the center emerges with just a few moist crumbs clinging to it.
Allow the brownies to cool before cutting into squares.
NUTRITION Calories: 276 | Fat: 14g | Carbs: 38g | Protein: 4g

Blueberry Muffins

Prep Time: 15 minutes
Cook Time: 20-25 minutes
Servings: 12 muffins
Ingredients:
2 teaspoon of baking powder
1/3 cup milk
1 teaspoon of vanilla extract
1/3 cup vegetable oil
1 1/2 cups all-purpose flour
3/4 cup granulated sugar
1/2 teaspoon of salt
1 egg
1 cup fresh or frozen blueberries

Directions:
Preheat your Ninja Foodi possible cooker pro to 350°F. In a large mixing bowl, combine the flour, sugar, salt, and baking powder.
In a separate bowl, mix together the vegetable oil, egg, milk, and vanilla extract.
Pour the wet ingredients into the dry ingredients and stir until just combined. Gently fold in the blueberries. Line a muffin tin with paper liners or grease it.
Fill each muffin cup about 2/3 full with the batter. Place the muffin tin in the cooker pro and bake for 20-25 minutes or until a toothpick inserted into the center of a muffin comes out clean.
Allow the muffins to cool for a few minutes before removing them from the tin.
NUTRITION Calories: 206 | Fat: 9g | Carbs: 30g | Protein: 3g

Lemon Bars

Prep Time: 20 minutes
Cook Time: 35-40 minutes
Servings: 16 bars
Ingredients:
1/4 cup powdered sugar
2 tablespoons of lemon juice
Zest of one lemon
2 large eggs
1 cup granulated sugar
1 cup all-purpose flour
1/2 cup unsalted butter, softened
2 tablespoons of all-purpose flour
1/2 teaspoon of baking powder
Powdered sugar for dusting

Directions:
Preheat your Ninja Foodi possible cooker pro to 350°F.
In a mixing bowl, combine 1 cup of flour, softened butter, and 1/4 cup of powdered sugar. Press this mixture into the bottom of a greased 8x8-inch baking pan.
Bake the crust for 15-20 minutes until it's lightly golden.
While the crust is baking, combine the eggs, granulated sugar, 2 tablespoons of flour, baking powder, lemon juice, and lemon zest in a separate bowl.
Pour this lemon mixture over the baked crust and return it to the cooker pro.
Bake for an additional 20-25 minutes or until the top is set and lightly browned.
Let the bars cool completely in the pan, then dust with powdered sugar before cutting into squares.
NUTRITION Calories: 159 | Fat: 7g | Carbs: 24g | Protein: 2g

Strawberry Shortcake

Prep Time: 20 minutes
Cook Time: 15-20 minutes
Servings: 6 servings
Ingredients:
For the Shortcake:
1 tablespoon baking powder
2/3 cup milk
1/2 teaspoon of salt
2 cups all-purpose flour
1/4 cup granulated sugar
1/2 cup unsalted butter, cold and cubed
1 teaspoon of vanilla extract
For the Strawberry Filling:
1/4 cup granulated sugar
Whipped cream for topping
4 cups fresh strawberries, hulled and sliced
Directions:
For the Shortcake:
Preheat your Ninja Foodi possible cooker pro to 400°F.

In a large mixing bowl, combine the flour, sugar, baking powder, and salt.
Add the cold, cubed butter to the flour mixture. Use a pastry cutter or your fingers to work the butter into the flour until it resembles coarse crumbs.
Pour in the milk and vanilla extract. Stir until the dough comes together.
Turn the dough out onto a floured surface and pat it into a rectangle about 1 inch thick. Use a round biscuit cutter or a glass to cut out shortcakes. Place them on a baking sheet lined with parchment paper.
Bake in the cooker pro for 15-20 minutes or until the shortcakes are golden brown.

For the Strawberry Filling:
In a bowl, combine the sliced strawberries and granulated sugar. Let them sit for about 15 minutes to release their juices.
To assemble, slice the shortcakes in half horizontally, spoon strawberries over the bottom half, and top with whipped cream. Place the other half of the shortcake on top.
NUTRITION Calories: 440 | Fat: 19g | Carbs: 64g | Protein: 5g

Banana Bread

Prep Time: 15 minutes
Cook Time: 45-55 minutes
Servings: 1 loaf
Ingredients:
1/3 cup melted unsalted butter
3/4 cup granulated sugar
1 1/2 cups all-purpose flour
2 to 3 ripe bananas, mashed
1 large egg, beaten
1 teaspoon of baking soda
1 teaspoon of vanilla extract
Salt (a pinch)
1/4 cup chopped walnuts or chocolate chips (optional)

Directions:
Set the Ninja Foodi possible cooker pro to 350 degrees Fahrenheit.
Use a fork to mash the ripe bananas in a mixing basin. The mashed bananas are combined with the melted butter.
Add a dash of salt and the baking soda. Mix thoroughly.
Add vanilla, sugar, and one egg that has been whisked.
Add the flour and blend just until combined. Add chopped walnuts or chocolate chips, as desired.
The batter should be poured into a dusted and buttered loaf pan.
A toothpick inserted in the center should come out clean after 45 to 55 minutes of baking in the cooker pro.
Before cutting the banana bread, let it cool.
NUTRITION Calories: 224 | Fat: 7g | Carbs: 38g | Protein: 3.5g

Pumpkin Bread

Prep Time: 15 minutes
Cook Time: 50-60 minutes
Servings: 1 loaf
Ingredients:
2 large eggs
1 cup canned pumpkin puree
1/4 teaspoon of ground ginger
1/2 cup unsalted butter, softened
1 teaspoon of baking soda
1/2 teaspoon of ground nutmeg
1/4 teaspoon of ground cloves
1 3/4 cups all-purpose flour
1 1/2 cups granulated sugar
1/2 teaspoon of salt
1/2 teaspoon of ground cinnamon
1/2 cup water

Directions:
Set the Ninja Foodi possible cooker pro to 350 degrees Fahrenheit. Mix the flour, baking soda, salt, and spices in a mixing dish.
The softened butter and granulated sugar should be creamed until frothy in a separate basin. Mix in the pumpkin puree after adding each egg one at a time.
Three portions of the dry ingredients should be added, alternating with the water. Start and end with the dry ingredients, then mix thoroughly.
The batter should be poured into a dusted and buttered loaf pan.
A toothpick inserted in the center should come out clean after baking the pan in the cooker pro for 50 to 60 minutes.
Before slicing, let the pumpkin bread cool.
NUTRITION Calories: 219 | Fat: 8g | Carbs: 35g | Protein: 3g

Raspberry Thumbprint Cookies

Prep Time: 20 minutes
Cook Time: 12-15 minutes
Servings: About 24 cookies
Ingredients:
2 large eggs
1/2 teaspoon of salt
1 cup finely chopped walnuts or pecans
2 teaspoon of vanilla extract
1 cup unsalted butter, softened
2/3 cup granulated sugar
2 1/2 cups all-purpose flour
1/2 cup raspberry jam or preserves

Directions:
Preheat your Ninja Foodi possible cooker pro to 350°F.
In a large mixing bowl, cream together the softened butter and granulated sugar.
Add the eggs one at a time, then stir in the vanilla extract.
In a separate bowl, combine the flour and salt. Gradually add this dry mixture to the wet ingredients, mixing until just combined.
Roll the dough into 1-inch balls. Roll each ball in chopped nuts.
Place the dough balls on a baking sheet lined with parchment paper. Make a thumbprint indentation in the center of each cookie.
Fill each indentation with raspberry jam or preserves.
Place the baking sheet in the cooker pro and bake for 12-15 minutes or until the cookies are lightly golden.
Allow the cookies to cool on a wire rack before serving.
NUTRITION Calories: 130 | Fat: 7g | Carbs: 16g | Protein: 2g

Cheesecake

Prep Time: 20 minutes
Cook Time: 40-45 minutes (plus cooling time
Servings: 8-10 slices
Ingredients:
For the Crust:
1/2 cup unsalted butter, melted
1 1/2 cups graham cracker crumbs
1/4 cup granulated sugar
For the Filling:
1 cup granulated sugar
1 teaspoon of vanilla extract
3 (8 oz) packages cream cheese, softened
3 large eggs
Directions:
For the Crust:
In a bowl, combine the graham cracker crumbs, sugar, and melted butter. Press the mixture into the bottom of a greased springform pan.
For the Filling:
In a separate bowl, beat the cream cheese until smooth. Add the sugar and vanilla extract, and beat until well combined.
Add the eggs one at a time, beating after each addition. Pour the cream cheese mixture over the crust in the pan.
Preheat your Ninja Foodi possible cooker pro to 325°F. Place the pan in the cooker pro and bake for 40-45 minutes, or until the edges are set, but the center is slightly jiggly.
Turn off the cooker pro and crack the lid open slightly. Let the cheesecake cool in the cooker for about 1 hour.
Remove the cheesecake from the cooker pro, refrigerate for several hours or overnight, and serve chilled.
NUTRITION Calories: 406 | Fat: 30g | Carbs: 29g | Protein: 6g

Carrot Cake

Prep Time: 20 minutes
Cook Time: 35-40 minutes
Servings: 12 slices
Ingredients:
For the Cake:
1 teaspoon of baking soda
1/2 teaspoon of ground ginger
1/2 cup unsalted butter, softened
2 cups grated carrots
1/2 cup crushed pineapple, drained
1 cup granulated sugar
1/2 cup brown sugar, packed
3 large eggs
1/2 teaspoon of salt
2 teaspoon of ground cinnamon
2 cups all-purpose flour
1 1/2 teaspoon of baking powder
1/2 teaspoon of ground nutmeg
1 teaspoon of vanilla extract
1/2 cup chopped walnuts or pecans (optional)

For the Cream Cheese Frosting:
8 oz cream cheese, softened
1/2 cup unsalted butter, softened
4 cups powdered sugar
1 teaspoon of vanilla extract

Directions:
For the Cake:
In a mixing bowl, blend together the baking powder, baking soda, salt, flour, and spices.
In a separate bowl, beat the softened butter, granulated sugar, and brown sugar until they achieve a light and fluffy consistency.
Add the eggs one at a time, ensuring thorough incorporation after each addition, and stir in the vanilla extract. Gradually introduce the dry ingredients into the wet mixture, stirring until just unified.
Gently fold in the grated carrots, crushed pineapple, and optionally, the chopped nuts.
Preheat your Ninja Foodi Possible Cooker Pro to 350°F. Grease and flour a cake pan that fits comfortably inside your cooker pro. Pour the batter into the prepared pan. Position the pan inside the cooker pro and bake for approximately 35-40 minutes, or until a toothpick inserted into the center emerges clean.

For the Cream Cheese Frosting:
In a mixing bowl, beat together the softened cream cheese, softened butter, powdered sugar, and vanilla extract until smooth and creamy.
Once the cake has cooled, spread the cream cheese frosting over the top.
NUTRITION Calories: 574 | Fat: 33g | Carbs: 54g | Protein: 6g

Chocolate Cake

Prep Time: 20 minutes
Cook Time: 25-30 minutes
Servings: 12 slices
Ingredients:
For the Cake:
1 teaspoon of salt
1 cup whole milk
3/4 cup unsweetened cocoa powder
1 3/4 cups granulated sugar
2 large eggs
1 1/2 teaspoon of baking powder
2 teaspoons of vanilla extract
1 1/2 teaspoon of baking soda
1/2 cup vegetable oil
1 cup boiling water
1 3/4 cups all-purpose flour

For the Chocolate Ganache (Optional:
8 oz semisweet chocolate, chopped
1 cup heavy cream

Directions:
For the Cake:
Preheat your Ninja Foodi possible cooker pro to 350°F. Grease and flour two 9-inch round cake pans.
In a large mixing bowl, combine the flour, sugar, cocoa powder, baking powder, baking soda, and salt.
Add the eggs, milk, vegetable oil, and vanilla extract. Beat on medium speed for 2 minutes.
Stir in the boiling water. The batter will be thin but that's okay.
Pour the batter evenly into the prepared pans.
Place the pans in the cooker pro and bake for 25-30 minutes, or until a toothpick inserted into the center comes out clean.

For the Chocolate Ganache (Optional:
Heat the heavy cream in a saucepan over medium heat until it begins to simmer.
Remove from heat and add the chopped chocolate. Let it sit for a minute, then whisk until smooth.
Let the ganache cool for a few minutes before pouring it over the cooled cake.

NUTRITION Calories: 297 | Fat: 14g | Carbs: 42g | Protein: 5g

Vanilla Cupcakes

Prep Time: 15 minutes
Cook Time: 15-20 minutes
Servings: 12 cupcakes
Ingredients:
For the Cupcakes:
2 teaspoons of vanilla extract
2 large eggs
1/2 cup whole milk
1/2 cup unsalted butter, softened
1 cup granulated sugar
1 1/2 cups all-purpose flour
1 1/2 teaspoon of baking powder
1/4 teaspoon of salt
For the Buttercream Frosting:
1 cup unsalted butter, softened
4 cups powdered sugar
2 teaspoons of vanilla extract
2-3 tablespoons of whole milk

Directions:
For the Cupcakes:
Preheat your Ninja Foodi possible cooker pro to 350°F.
Line a muffin tin with cupcake liners.
In a bowl, combine the baking powder, flour, and salt.
In a separate bowl, cream together the softened butter and granulated sugar.
Add the eggs one at a time, beating well after each addition. Stir in the vanilla extract.
Gradually pour the dry ingredients into the wet ingredients, (alternate with the whole milk) beginning and ending with the dry ingredients. Mix until just combined.
Divide the batter evenly among the cupcake liners.
Place the muffin tin in the cooker pro and bake for 15-20 minutes or until a toothpick inserted into the center of a cupcake comes out clean.

For the Buttercream Frosting:
In a clean mixing bowl, whisk the butter until smooth and creamy.
Add the vanilla extract, sugar, and enough milk to achieve your desired consistency. Beat until smooth and fluffy.
Once the cupcakes have cooled, frost them with the buttercream frosting.

NUTRITION Calories: 269 | Fat: 12g | Carbs: 39g | Protein: 2g

Gingerbread Cookies

Prep Time: 30 minutes
Chill Time: 2 hours
Cook Time: 8-10 minutes
Servings: Varies (depending on cookie cutter size)
Ingredients:
For the Cookies:
1/4 teaspoon of ground cloves
3/4 cup granulated sugar
1 large egg
1/2 cup molasses
1/4 teaspoon of ground nutmeg
3 cups all-purpose flour
1 1/2 teaspoon of ground ginger
1 1/2 teaspoon of ground cinnamon
3/4 teaspoon of baking soda
1/2 teaspoon of salt
3/4 cup unsalted butter, softened

For the Royal Icing (Optional):
1 1/2 cups powdered sugar
2 tablespoons of meringue powder
3 tablespoons of warm water

Directions:
For the Cookies:
In a bowl, combine the flour, ground ginger, ground cinnamon, ground cloves, ground nutmeg, baking soda, and salt.
In another bowl, cream together the softened butter and granulated sugar.
Beat in the egg and molasses.
Gradually add the dry ingredients to the wet ingredients, mixing until just combined.
Divide the dough in half, shape each half into a disc, wrap in plastic wrap, and chill in the refrigerator for at least 2 hours.
Preheat your Ninja Foodi possible cooker pro to 350°F.
Roll out the chilled dough on a floured surface to your desired thickness. Use gingerbread cookie cutters to cut out shapes.
Place the cookie shapes on a baking sheet lined with parchment paper.
Bake in the cooker pro for 8-10 minutes or until the edges are lightly golden.
Let the cookies cool on a wire rack.

For the Royal Icing (Optional):
In a bowl, combine the powdered sugar, meringue powder, and warm water. Beat until smooth and thick.
Use the royal icing to decorate the cooled gingerbread cookies as desired.

NUTRITION Calories: 181 | Fat: 5g | Carbs: 31g | Protein: 2g

Red Velvet Cake

Prep Time: 20 minutes
Cook Time: 25-30 minutes
Servings: 12 slices
Ingredients:
For the Cake:
1 teaspoon of baking powder
2 large eggs, room temperature
2 tablespoons of red food coloring
1 teaspoon of vanilla extract
2 1/2 cups all-purpose flour
1 1/2 cups granulated sugar
1 teaspoon of salt
1 1/2 teaspoon of unsweetened cocoa powder
1 teaspoon of baking soda
1 1/2 cups vegetable oil
1 cup buttermilk, room temperature
1 teaspoon of white vinegar
Cream cheese frosting (store-bought or homemade)

Directions:
For the Cake:
Preheat your Ninja Foodi possible cooker pro to 350°F.
Grease and flour two 9-inch round cake pans.
In a large mixing bowl, combine the baking powder, flour, baking soda, sugar, salt, and cocoa powder.
In a separate bowl, combine the vegetable oil, buttermilk, eggs, food coloring, vanilla extract, and white vinegar.
Gradually add the wet ingredients to the dry ones, mixing until just combined.
Divide the batter evenly between the prepared pans.
Place the pans in the cooker pro and bake for 25-30 minutes or until a toothpick comes out clean.
Let the cakes cool in the pans for a few minutes, then remove them from the pans and let them cool completely on a wire rack.
Once the cakes are cool, frost with cream cheese frosting.

NUTRITION Calories: 370 | Fat: 20g | Carbs: 43g | Protein: 5g

Peanut Butter Cookies

Prep Time: 15 minutes
Cook Time: 10-12 minutes
Servings: About 24 cookies
Ingredients:
1 large egg
1 teaspoon of vanilla extract
1 1/4 cups all-purpose flour
1/2 cup packed brown sugar
1/2 cup creamy peanut butter
1/2 cup unsalted butter, softened
1/2 cup granulated sugar
1/2 teaspoon of baking powder
1/2 teaspoon of baking soda
1/4 teaspoon of salt

Directions:
Preheat your Ninja Foodi possible cooker pro to 375°F.
In a large mixing bowl, cream together the softened butter, granulated sugar, brown sugar, and peanut butter until smooth. Beat in the egg and vanilla extract.
In a separate bowl, combine the flour, baking powder, baking soda, and salt. Gradually add this dry mixture to the wet ingredients, mixing until just combined.
Roll the dough into 1-inch balls and place them on a baking sheet lined with parchment paper.
Flatten each ball with a fork to create a crisscross pattern.
Bake in the cooker pro for 10-12 minutes or until the edges are golden. Allow the cookies to cool on a wire rack.

NUTRITION Calories: 148 | Fat: 8g | Carbs: 17g | Protein: 3g

Oatmeal Raisin Cookies

Prep Time: 20 minutes
Cook Time: 10-12 minutes
Servings: About 24 cookies
Ingredients:
1/2 cup packed brown sugar
1 large egg
1 cup all-purpose flour
1 1/2 cups old-fashioned rolled oats
1/2 teaspoon of baking soda
1/2 teaspoon of ground cinnamon
1 teaspoon of vanilla extract
1/4 teaspoon of salt
1/2 cup unsalted butter, softened
1/2 cup granulated sugar
1 cup raisins

Directions:
Preheat your Ninja Foodi possible cooker pro to 350°F.
In a large mixing bowl, cream together the softened butter, granulated sugar, and brown sugar until smooth.
Beat in the egg and vanilla extract.
In a separate bowl, combine the flour, baking soda, ground cinnamon, and salt. Gradually add this dry mixture to the wet ingredients, mixing until just combined. Stir in the rolled oats and raisins.
Drop spoonfuls of cookie dough onto a baking sheet lined with parchment paper.
Bake in the cooker pro for 10-12 minutes or until the edges are golden.
Let the cookies cool on a wire rack.

NUTRITION Calories: 122 | Fat: 4g | Carbs: 20g | Protein: 2g

Coconut Macaroons

Prep Time: 15 minutes
Cook Time: 20-25 minutes
Servings: About 24 macaroons
Ingredients:
1/2 teaspoon of almond extract
1/4 teaspoon of salt
4 large egg whites
1/2 cup granulated sugar
1 (14 oz) package sweetened shredded coconut

Directions:
Preheat your Ninja Foodi possible cooker pro to 325°F.
In a heatproof mixing bowl, combine the egg whites, granulated sugar, almond extract, and salt.
Place the mixing bowl over a saucepan of simmering water (double boiler). Stir constantly until the mixture is warm to the touch and the sugar has dissolved.
Remove the bowl from the heat and stir in the shredded coconut.
Drop spoonfuls of the mixture onto a baking sheet lined with parchment paper.
Bake in the cooker pro for 20-25 minutes or until the macaroons are golden brown on the outside.
Allow the macaroons to cool on a wire rack.

NUTRITION Calories: 57 | Fat: 3g | Carbs: 7g | Protein: 1g

Chocolate Babka

Prep Time: 30 minutes
Cook Time: 30-35 minutes
Servings: 1 loaf
Ingredients:
For the Dough:
2 1/4 teaspoon of active dry yeast
1/2 teaspoon of salt
3 1/4 cups all-purpose flour
1/4 cup granulated sugar
1/2 cup whole milk
1/4 cup unsalted butter
2 large eggs

For the Filling:
1/2 cup cocoa powder
1/2 teaspoon of ground cinnamon
1/2 cup unsalted butter, melted
1/2 cup granulated sugar
1/2 cup semisweet chocolate chips (optional)

Directions:
For the Dough:
In a large mixing bowl, combine 3 cups of flour, granulated sugar, yeast, and salt.
In a small saucepan, heat the milk and butter over low heat until the butter is melted. Remove from heat and let it cool lukewarm.
Pour the milk mixture into the dry ingredients and stir until it forms a dough.
Add the eggs and the remaining 1/4 cup of flour. Knead the dough until it's smooth and elastic.
Place the dough in a greased bowl, cover with a clean cloth, and let it rise for about 1 hour or until it has doubled in size.

For the Filling:
In a bowl, mix together the melted butter, granulated sugar, cocoa powder, and ground cinnamon.
Preheat your Ninja Foodi possible cooker pro to 350°F.
Roll out the dough into a large rectangle.
Spread the filling mixture evenly over the dough.
Sprinkle chocolate chips if desired.
Roll up the dough tightly, starting from the long side.
Cut the roll in half lengthwise, exposing the layers.
Twist the two halves together to create a braided effect.
Place the dough in a greased loaf pan.
Bake in the cooker pro for 30-35 minutes or until it's golden brown and cooked through.
Let the babka cool before slicing and serving.

NUTRITION Calories: 249 | Fat: 10g | Carbs: 35g | Protein: 5g

CHAPTER FIVE

SEAR/SAUTE RECIPES

Lemon Garlic Butter Chicken

Prep Time: 10 minutes
Cook Time: 20 minutes
Servings: 4
Ingredients:
4 boneless, skinless chicken breasts
Salt and pepper to taste
2 tablespoons of olive oil
4 cloves garlic, minced
1 lemon, juiced and zested
1/2 cup chicken broth
2 tablespoons of butter
Fresh parsley, chopped, for garnish

Directions:
Season both sides of the chicken breasts with salt and pepper.
Select the "Sear/Saute" setting on your Ninja Foodi food cooker pro and heat the olive oil.
Sear the chicken breasts for 4-5 minutes per side, or until golden brown. Take them out and set them aside.
In the same cooker, sauté the minced garlic for about 1 minute, or until fragrant.
Combine the lemon juice, lemon zest, and chicken broth in a mixing bowl. To blend, stir everything together.
Return the seared chicken breasts to the pot and cook for about 10 minutes, or until the chicken is well cooked.
To make a creamy lemon garlic sauce, stir in the butter.
Serve garnished with chopped fresh parsley.
NUTRITION Calories: 378 | Fat: 19g | Carbs: 5g | Protein: 46g

Beef and Broccoli Stir-Fry

Prep Time: 15 minutes
Cook Time: 15 minutes
Servings: 4
Ingredients:
1 pound flank steak, thinly sliced
Salt and pepper to taste
2 tablespoons of vegetable oil
2 cups broccoli florets
1/2 cup soy sauce
2 tablespoons of brown sugar
2 cloves garlic, minced
1 teaspoon of ginger, grated
2 tablespoons of cornstarch
Cooked rice, for serving

Sesame seeds, for garnish (optional)

Directions:
Season the sliced flank steak with salt and pepper.
In your Ninja Foodi possible cooker pro, select the "Sear/Saute" function and heat the vegetable oil.
Sear the beef slices for about 2-3 minutes until they are browned. Remove and set aside.
Add the broccoli florets to the cooker and sauté for about 2 minutes until they begin to soften.
In a bowl, combine soy sauce, brown sugar, minced garlic, grated ginger, and cornstarch.
Pour the sauce mixture into the cooker with the broccoli and stir to combine.
Return the seared beef to the pot and simmer for about 5 minutes until the sauce thickens and the beef is heated through.
Serve the beef and broccoli stir-fry over cooked rice and garnish with sesame seeds if desired.
NUTRITION Calories: 305 | Fat: 18g | Carbs: 11g | Protein: 25g

Lemon Butter Garlic Shrimp

Prep Time: 10 minutes
Cook Time: 5 minutes
Servings: 4
Ingredients:
1 pound large shrimp, peeled and deveined
Salt and pepper to taste
2 tablespoons of butter
4 cloves garlic, minced
Juice and zest of 1 lemon
Fresh parsley, chopped, for garnish

Directions:
Season the shrimp with salt and pepper.
In your Ninja Foodi possible cooker pro, select the "Sear/Saute" function and melt the butter.
Add the minced garlic and sauté for about 1 minute until fragrant.
Add the shrimp to the cooker and cook for about 2-3 minutes per side until they turn pink and opaque.
Stir in the lemon juice and lemon zest to create a flavorful lemon garlic butter sauce.
Garnish with chopped fresh parsley and serve.
NUTRITION Calories: 233 | Fat: 14g | Carbs: 4g | Protein: 23g

Sautéed Spinach with Garlic

Prep Time: 5 minutes
Cook Time: 5 minutes
Servings: 4
Ingredients:
1 pound fresh spinach leaves
2 tablespoons of olive oil
4 cloves garlic, minced
Salt and pepper to taste
Lemon wedges, for garnish (optional)

Directions:
Select the "Sear/Saute" setting on your Ninja Foodi food cooker pro and heat the olive oil.
Sauté the minced garlic for about 1 minute, or until fragrant.
Sauté the fresh spinach leaves in the cooker for 2-3 minutes, or until they wilt and become tender.
Season to taste with salt and pepper.
To enhance flavor, serve the sautéed spinach with optional lemon wedges.

NUTRITION Calories: 87 | Fat: 7g | Carbs: 4g | Protein: 2g

Ratatouille

Prep Time: 15 minutes
Cook Time: 25 minutes
Servings: 6
Ingredients:
1 eggplant, diced
2 zucchinis, diced
2 yellow bell peppers, diced
1 red onion, diced
4 cloves garlic, minced
2 cups diced tomatoes (canned or fresh)
2 tablespoons of olive oil
1 teaspoon of dried thyme
1 teaspoon of dried basil
Salt and pepper to taste
Fresh basil, chopped, for garnish

Directions:
In your Ninja Foodi possible cooker pro, select the "Sear/Saute" function and heat the olive oil.
Add the diced eggplant, zucchinis, bell peppers, red onion, and minced garlic. Sauté for about 5 minutes until they begin to soften.
Stir in the diced tomatoes, dried thyme, and dried basil. Season with salt and pepper to taste.
Cover and simmer for about 20 minutes, stirring occasionally, until the vegetables are tender.
Garnish with chopped fresh basil before serving.
NUTRITION Calories: 98 | Fat: 7g | Carbs: 10g | Protein: 2g

Chicken and Rice Casserole

Prep Time: 15 minutes
Cook Time: 2 hours
Servings: 6
Ingredients:
4 boneless, skinless chicken breasts
Salt and pepper to taste
1 tablespoon olive oil
1 onion, chopped
2 cloves garlic, minced
1 cup long-grain white rice
2 cups chicken broth
1 cup mixed vegetables (frozen or fresh)
1 teaspoon of dried thyme
1 teaspoon of paprika
1/2 cup shredded cheddar cheese

Directions:
Season both sides of the chicken breasts with salt and pepper.
Select the "Sear/Saute" setting on your Ninja Foodi food cooker pro and heat the olive oil.
Sear the chicken breasts for 3-4 minutes per side, or until golden brown. Take out and set aside.
Add chopped onion and minced garlic to the same cooker. Cook for 2 minutes, or until the onion is transparent.
Stir in the rice and cook for 2 minutes more, or until it's lightly browned.
Combine the chicken broth, mixed vegetables, dried thyme, and paprika in a mixing bowl. To blend, stir everything together.
Put the seared chicken breasts back in the pot.
Close the lid of the cooker and select "Slow Cook." Cook on high settings until done.
Fluff the rice with a fork and top with grated cheddar cheese.
Serve the chicken slices over the cheesy rice.

NUTRITION Calories: 379 | Fat: 14g | Carbs: 30g | Protein: 32g

Lemon Butter Garlic Shrimp

Prep Time: 10 minutes
Cook Time: 5 minutes
Servings: 4
Ingredients:
1 pound large shrimp, peeled and deveined
Salt and pepper to taste
2 tablespoons of butter
4 cloves garlic, minced
Juice and zest of 1 lemon
Fresh parsley, chopped, for garnish

Directions:
Season the shrimp with salt and pepper.
In your Ninja Foodi possible cooker pro, select the "Sear/Saute" function and melt the butter.
Add the minced garlic and sauté for about 1 minute until fragrant.
Add the shrimp to the cooker and cook for about 2-3 minutes per side until they turn pink and opaque.
Stir in the lemon juice and lemon zest to create a flavorful lemon garlic butter sauce.
Garnish with chopped fresh parsley and serve.

NUTRITION Calories: 233| Fat: 13g | Carbs: 4g | Protein: 23g

Chicken Piccata

Prep Time: 15 minutes
Cook Time: 20 minutes
Servings: 4
Ingredients:
4 boneless, skinless chicken breasts
Salt and pepper to taste
1/2 cup all-purpose flour, for dredging
2 tablespoons of olive oil
4 cloves garlic, minced
1/2 cup chicken broth
1/2 cup dry white wine
Juice of 1 lemon
2 tablespoons of capers
2 tablespoons of butter
Fresh parsley, chopped, for garnish

Directions:
Season the chicken breasts with salt and pepper.
Dredge the chicken breasts in flour, shaking off excess.
In your Ninja Foodi possible cooker pro, select the "Sear/Saute" function and heat the olive oil.
Sear the chicken breasts for about 4-5 minutes per side until they are golden brown and cooked through. Remove them and set aside.
In the same cooker, add minced garlic and sauté for about 1 minute until fragrant.

Pour in the chicken broth, dry white wine, and lemon juice. Add capers and stir to combine.
Return the chicken breasts to the pot and simmer for about 5 minutes.
Stir in the butter to create a rich, lemony sauce.
Garnish with chopped fresh parsley and serve.

NUTRITION Calories: 398 | Fat: 18g | Carbs: 16g | Protein: 38g

Chicken and Vegetable Stir-Fry

Prep Time: 15 minutes
Cook Time: 15 minutes
Servings: 4
Ingredients:
1 pound boneless, skinless chicken breasts, cut into strips
Salt and pepper to taste
2 tablespoons of vegetable oil
2 cups broccoli florets
1 red bell pepper, sliced
1 cup snow peas
1 carrot, julienned
1/2 cup soy sauce
2 tablespoons of honey
2 cloves garlic, minced
1 teaspoon of ginger, grated
2 tablespoons of cornstarch

Directions:
Season the chicken strips with salt and pepper.
In your Ninja Foodi possible cooker pro, select the "Sear/Saute" function and heat the vegetable oil.
Sear the chicken strips for about 3-4 minutes until they are cooked through. Remove them and set aside.
Add the broccoli, red bell pepper, snow peas, and julienned carrot to the cooker. Sauté for about 3-4 minutes until the vegetables are tender-crisp.
In a clean bowl, mix the garlic, soy sauce, honey, ginger, and cornstarch.
Pour the mixture into the Ninja cooker with the sautéed vegetables.
Return the cooked chicken to the pot and stir to combine.
Simmer for another 2-3 minutes until the sauce thickens.
Serve the chicken and vegetable stir-fry hot.

NUTRITION Calories: 394 | Fat: 16g | Carbs: 25g | Protein: 35g

Beef Tacos

Prep Time: 15 minutes
Cook Time: 15 minutes
Servings: 4
Ingredients:
1 pound ground beef
1 onion, chopped
2 cloves garlic, minced
1 packet taco seasoning mix
1 cup tomato sauce
1 cup water
8 small taco shells
Shredded lettuce, diced tomatoes, shredded cheese, sour cream, for toppings

Directions:
In your Ninja Foodi possible cooker pro, select the "Sear/Saute" function and heat a bit of olive oil.
Add chopped onion and minced garlic. Sauté for about 2 minutes until the onion is translucent.
Add ground beef and cook until browned, breaking it up with a spoon as it cooks.
Stir in the taco seasoning mix, tomato sauce, and water. Simmer for about 5 minutes until the sauce thickens.
Serve the beef taco filling in taco shells, and top with shredded lettuce, diced tomatoes, shredded cheese, and sour cream.
NUTRITION Calories: 494 | Fat: 24g | Carbs: 33g | Protein: 35g

Chicken Alfredo

Prep Time: 10 minutes
Cook Time: 20 minutes
Servings: 4
Ingredients:
4 boneless, skinless chicken breasts
Salt and pepper to taste
2 tablespoons of olive oil
1/2 cup diced onion
2 cloves garlic, minced
1 cup heavy cream
1 cup grated Parmesan cheese
1 teaspoon of Italian seasoning
Cooked fettuccine pasta, for serving
Fresh parsley, chopped, for garnish

Directions:
Sprinkle the chicken breasts with enough salt and pepper (to taste).
In your Ninja Foodi possible cooker pro, select the "Sear/Saute" function and heat the olive oil.
Sear the chicken breasts for about 4-5 minutes per side. Remove them and set aside.

In the same cooker, add diced onion and minced garlic. Sauté for about 2 minutes until the onion is translucent.
Pour in the heavy cream and stir to combine.
Add the grated Parmesan cheese and Italian seasoning. Stir until the sauce thickens.
Return the cooked chicken breasts to the pot and simmer for an additional 5 minutes.
Serve the chicken Alfredo over cooked fettuccine pasta and garnish with chopped fresh parsley.
NUTRITION Calories: 648 | Fat: 41g | Carbs: 16g | Protein: 49g

Beef Fajitas

Prep Time: 15 minutes
Cook Time: 15 minutes
Servings: 4
Ingredients:
1 pound flank steak, thinly sliced
Salt and pepper to taste
2 tablespoons of vegetable oil
1 onion, sliced
1 red bell pepper, sliced
1 green bell pepper, sliced
2 cloves garlic, minced
1 teaspoon of chili powder
1 teaspoon of ground cumin
1 teaspoon of paprika
Flour tortillas, for serving
Sour cream, salsa, and guacamole, for toppings

Directions:
Sprinkle the sliced flank steak with salt and pepper. In your Ninja Foodi possible cooker pro, select the "Sear/Saute" function and heat the vegetable oil. Sear the steak slices for about 2-3 mins per side until they are browned. Remove them and set aside. In the same cooker, add sliced onion and bell peppers. Sauté for about 3-4 minutes until they begin to soften. Add minced garlic, chili powder, ground cumin, and paprika. Stir to coat the vegetables with the spices. Return the seared steak to the pot and cook for an additional 2-3 minutes until heated through.
Serve the beef fajita mixture in flour tortillas and top with sour cream, salsa, and guacamole.
NUTRITION Calories: 405 | Fat: 22g | Carbs: 17g | Protein: 34g

Lemon Butter Garlic Scallops

Prep Time: 10 minutes
Cook Time: 5 minutes
Servings: 4
Ingredients:
1 pound large sea scallops
Salt and pepper to taste
2 tablespoons of butter
4 cloves garlic, minced
Juice and zest of 1 lemon
Fresh parsley, chopped, for garnish

Directions:
Sprinkle the scallops with salt and pepper.
In your Ninja Foodi possible cooker pro, select the "Sear/Saute" function and melt the butter.
Add the minced garlic and sauté for about 1 min until fragrant.
Add the scallops to the cooker and cook for about 1-2 mins per side until they are lightly browned and opaque.
Stir in the lemon juice and lemon zest to create a flavorful lemon garlic butter sauce.
Garnish with chopped fresh parsley and serve.
NUTRITION Calories: 226 | Fat: 10g | Carbs: 5g | Protein: 29g

Vegetarian Stir-Fried Rice

Prep Time: 15 minutes
Cook Time: 15 minutes
Servings: 4
Ingredients:
2 cups cooked jasmine rice, cooled
2 tablespoons of vegetable oil
1 onion, chopped
2 cloves garlic, minced
1 cup mixed vegetables (frozen or fresh)
2 tablespoons of soy sauce
1 tablespoon oyster sauce (optional)
1/2 teaspoon of sesame oil
Scrambled eggs, chopped green onions, and sesame seeds, for garnish

Directions:
In your Ninja Foodi possible cooker pro, select the "Sear/Saute" function and heat the vegetable oil.
Add chopped onion and minced garlic. Sauté for about 2 mins until the onion is translucent.
Stir in the mixed vegetables and sauté for another 2-3 mins until they are heated through.
Add the cooked jasmine rice to the cooker and stir to combine.

In a bowl, mix together soy sauce, oyster sauce (if using), and sesame oil.
Pour the sauce mixture over the rice and stir-fry for an additional 3-4 minutes.
Serve the vegetarian stir-fried rice, garnished with scrambled eggs, chopped green onions, and sesame seeds.
NUTRITION Calories: 320 | Fat: 11g | Carbs: 47g | Protein: 7g

Chicken and Dumplings

Prep Time: 15 minutes
Cook Time: 30 minutes
Servings: 6
Ingredients:
4 boneless, skinless chicken breasts
Salt and pepper to taste
2 tablespoons of olive oil
1 onion, chopped
2 cloves garlic, minced
4 cups chicken broth
2 cups water
2 cups all-purpose flour
2 teaspoon of baking powder
1/2 cup milk
1 cup frozen peas and carrots
Fresh parsley, chopped, for garnish

Directions:
Sprinkle the chicken breasts with salt and pepper.
In your Ninja Foodi possible cooker pro, select the "Sear/Saute" function and heat the olive oil.
Sear the chicken breasts for about 4-5 mins per side until they are golden brown. Remove them and set aside.
In the same cooker, add onion and garlic, then sauté for about 2 mins.
Add the chicken broth and water. Bring to a simmer. In a bowl, mix together all-purpose flour, baking powder, and milk to form a dough.
Drop spoonfuls of the dough into the simmering broth to create dumplings.
Return the seared chicken to the pot and add frozen peas and carrots.
Simmer for about 15-20 mins until the dumplings are cooked through.
Garnish with chopped fresh parsley and serve.

NUTRITION Calories: 438 | Fat: 14g | Carbs: 46g | Protein: 29g

Lemon Butter Garlic Asparagus

Prep Time: 5 minutes
Cook Time: 10 minutes
Servings: 4
Ingredients:

1 bunch asparagus spears, trimmed
2 tablespoons of butter
4 cloves garlic, minced
Juice and zest of 1 lemon
Salt and pepper to taste

Directions:

In your Ninja Foodi possible cooker pro, select the "Sear/Saute" function and melt the butter.
Add minced garlic and sauté for about 1 minute until fragrant.
Add the trimmed asparagus spears to the cooker and sauté for about 5-7 minutes until they are tender-crisp.
Stir in the lemon juice and lemon zest to create a flavorful lemon garlic butter sauce.
Season with salt and pepper to taste.
Serve the lemon butter garlic asparagus hot.

NUTRITION Calories: 88 | Fat: 7g | Carbs: 5g | Protein: 3g

Cajun Shrimp and Grits

Prep Time: 15 minutes
Cook Time: 20 minutes
Servings: 4
Ingredients:

1 pound large shrimp, peeled and deveined
Salt and cayenne pepper to taste
2 tablespoons of butter
4 cloves garlic, minced
1 red bell pepper, chopped
1 green bell pepper, chopped
1 onion, chopped
2 cups chicken broth
1 cup quick-cooking grits
1 cup shredded cheddar cheese
Fresh parsley, chopped, for garnish

Directions:

Sprinkle the shrimp with salt and cayenne pepper.
In your Ninja Foodi possible cooker pro, select the "Sear/Saute" function and heat the butter.
Add minced garlic, chopped red and green bell peppers, and onion. Sauté for about 5 mins until the vegetables are softened.
Add the shrimp to the cooker and cook for about 2-3 mins per side until they turn pink and opaque.

Remove them and set aside.
Pour in the chicken broth and bring it to a simmer.
Stir in the quick-cooking grits and cook for about 5 minutes, stirring constantly until the grits are creamy.
Stir in the shredded cheddar cheese until melted.
Serve the Cajun shrimp over the cheesy grits and garnish with chopped fresh parsley.

NUTRITION Calories: 510 | Fat: 24g | Carbs: 42g | Protein: 31g

Thai Red Curry Shrimp

Prep Time: 15 minutes
Cook Time: 15 minutes
Servings: 4
Ingredients:

1 pound large shrimp, peeled and deveined
Salt and pepper to taste
2 tablespoons of red curry paste
1 can (14 ounces) coconut milk
1 red bell pepper, sliced
1 zucchini, sliced
1 carrot, julienned
2 tablespoons of fish sauce
1 tablespoon brown sugar
Cooked jasmine rice, for serving
Fresh cilantro leaves, for garnish

Directions:

Sprinkle the shrimp with salt and pepper.
In your Ninja Foodi possible cooker pro, select the "Sear/Saute" function and heat a bit of vegetable oil.
Add the red curry paste and sauté for about 1 min until fragrant.
Add the coconut milk and stir properly.
Add sliced red bell pepper, sliced zucchini, and julienned carrot.
Stir in fish sauce and brown sugar. Simmer for about 5 minutes until the vegetables are tender.
Add the seasoned shrimp to the pot and cook for about 2-3 minutes per side until they turn pink and opaque.
Serve the Thai red curry shrimp over cooked jasmine rice and garnish with fresh cilantro leaves.

NUTRITION Calories: 370 | Fat: 22g | Carbs: 21g | Protein: 25g

Chicken Marsala

Prep Time: 15 minutes
Cook Time: 25 minutes
Servings: 4
Ingredients:
4 boneless, skinless chicken breasts
Salt and pepper to taste
2 tablespoons of olive oil
8 ounces mushrooms, sliced
2 cloves garlic, minced
1 cup Marsala wine
1 cup chicken broth
2 tablespoons of butter
Fresh parsley, chopped, for garnish

Directions:
Sprinkle the chicken breasts with salt and pepper.
In your Ninja Foodi possible cooker pro, select the "Sear/Saute" function and heat the olive oil.
Sear the chicken breasts for about 4-5 minutes per side until they are golden brown. Remove them and set aside.
In the same cooker, add sliced mushrooms and minced garlic. Sauté for about 5 minutes until the mushrooms release their moisture and brown.
Pour in Marsala wine and chicken broth. Stir to combine.
Return the seared chicken to the pot and simmer for about 10 minutes until the chicken is cooked through.
Stir in the butter to create a rich Marsala sauce.
Garnish with chopped fresh parsley and serve.

NUTRITION Calories: 362 | Fat: 14g | Carbs: 8g | Protein: 33g

Beef and Mushroom Risotto

Prep Time: 10 minutes
Cook Time: 25 minutes
Servings: 4
Ingredients:
1 pound beef sirloin or tenderloin, thinly sliced into strips
Salt and black pepper to taste
2 tablespoons of olive oil
1 onion, chopped
2 cloves garlic, minced
8 ounces mushrooms, sliced
1 1/2 cups Arborio rice
1/2 cup dry white wine
4 cups beef broth, heated
1 cup grated Parmesan cheese
Fresh parsley, chopped, for garnish

Directions:
Season the beef strips with salt and black pepper.
In your Ninja Foodi possible cooker pro, select the "Sear/Saute" function and heat the olive oil.

Sear the beef strips for about 2-3 minutes until they are browned. Remove them and set aside.
In the same cooker, add chopped onion and minced garlic. Sauté for about 2 minutes until the onion is translucent.
Add the sliced mushrooms and continue to cook for another 3 minutes until they release their moisture and brown.
Stir in Arborio rice and cook for 2-3 minutes until it's lightly toasted.
Pour in the dry white wine and cook until it's mostly absorbed by the rice.
Add the heated beef broth, one cup at a time, stirring constantly and allowing it to be absorbed before adding more. Continue this process until the rice is tender and creamy. Return the seared beef to the pot and stir in the grated Parmesan cheese.
Garnish with chopped fresh parsley before serving.

NUTRITION Calories: 564 | Fat: 22g | Carbs: 51g | Protein: 33g

Pork Chops with Mushroom Gravy

Prep Time: 15 minutes
Cook Time: 30 minutes
Servings: 4
Ingredients:
4 bone-in pork chops
Salt and black pepper to taste
2 tablespoons of olive oil
8 ounces mushrooms, sliced
1 onion, chopped
2 cloves garlic, minced
2 cups chicken broth
1/2 cup heavy cream
1 teaspoon of dried thyme
Fresh parsley, chopped, for garnish

Directions:
Season the pork chops with salt and black pepper.
In your Ninja Foodi possible cooker pro, select the "Sear/Saute" function and heat the olive oil.
Sear the pork chops for about 3-4 minutes per side until they are browned. Remove them and set aside.
In the same cooker, add sliced mushrooms, chopped onion, and minced garlic. Sauté for about 5 minutes until the mushrooms are browned.
Pour in the chicken broth and heavy cream. Stir to combine.
Return the seared pork chops to the pot and sprinkle dried thyme over them.
Simmer for about 10-15 minutes until the pork chops are cooked through.
Garnish with chopped fresh parsley before serving.

NUTRITION Calories: 482 | Fat: 32g | Carbs: 11g | Protein: 34g

Chicken Enchiladas

Prep Time: 20 minutes
Cook Time: 25 minutes
Servings: 4
Ingredients:
2 cups shredded cooked chicken
Salt and black pepper to taste
2 tablespoons of vegetable oil
1 onion, chopped
2 cloves garlic, minced
1 can (10 ounces) red enchilada sauce
1/2 cup sour cream
1 cup shredded cheddar cheese
8 small flour tortillas
Sliced green onions and chopped cilantro, for garnish

Directions:
Season the shredded chicken with salt and black pepper.
In your Ninja Foodi possible cooker pro, select the "Sear/Saute" function and heat the vegetable oil.
Add chopped onion and minced garlic. Sauté for about 2 minutes until the onion is translucent.
Stir in the shredded chicken, half of the enchilada sauce, and sour cream. Mix until well combined.
Preheat your oven to 375°F (190°C).
Fill each flour tortilla with the chicken mixture, roll it up, and place it seam-side down in the cooker.
Pour the remaining enchilada sauce over the rolled tortillas and sprinkle shredded cheddar cheese on top.
Close the cooker's lid and select the "Bake" function.
Bake for about 15 minutes until the enchiladas are heated through and the cheese is bubbly.
Garnish with sliced green onions and chopped cilantro before serving.

NUTRITION Calories: 558 | Fat: 29g | Carbs: 38g | Protein: 37g

Creamy Spinach and Artichoke Dip

Prep Time: 10 minutes
Cook Time: 15 minutes
Servings: 8
Ingredients:
1 (10-ounce) package frozen chopped spinach, thawed and drained
1 (14-ounce) can artichoke hearts, drained and chopped
1 cup cream cheese
1/2 cup sour cream
1/2 cup mayonnaise
1 cup grated Parmesan cheese
1 cup shredded mozzarella cheese
2 cloves garlic, minced
Salt and black pepper to taste
Tortilla chips or baguette slices, for dipping

Directions:
In your Ninja Foodi possible cooker pro, select the "Sear/Saute" function and heat the cream cheese until it's softened.
Stir in the sour cream, mayonnaise, grated Parmesan cheese, shredded mozzarella cheese, minced garlic, and season with salt and black pepper.
Add the chopped spinach and chopped artichoke hearts. Stir to combine.
Continue to cook and stir until the dip is heated through and the cheeses are melted and bubbly.
Serve the creamy spinach and artichoke dip with tortilla chips or baguette slices for dipping.

NUTRITION Calories: 267 | Fat: 21g | Carbs: 9g | Protein: 11g

CHAPTER SIX
BRAISE RECIPES

Braised Short Ribs

Prep Time: 15 minutes
Cooking Time: 1 hour 30 minutes
Servings: 4
Ingredients:
4 bone-in beef short ribs
2 tablespoons of olive oil
1 onion, chopped
2 carrots, chopped
2 celery stalks, chopped
4 cloves garlic, minced
1 cup red wine
2 cups beef broth
2 sprigs rosemary
Salt and pepper to taste

Directions:
Season the short ribs with salt and pepper.
Select the "Braise" function on your Ninja Foodi and set it to high heat. Add olive oil and sear the short ribs until browned on all sides. Remove and set aside.
In the same pot, add chopped onions, carrots, celery, and garlic. Sauté for 5 minutes until softened.
Pour in red wine and simmer for 5 minutes to deglaze the pot.
Return the short ribs to the pot, add beef broth and rosemary sprigs.
Close the lid and set the Ninja Foodi to braise on low for 1 hour 30 minutes, then cook.
Once done, remove the short ribs and strain the sauce. Simmer the sauce to thicken.
Serve the short ribs with the sauce over mashed potatoes or polenta.
NUTRITION Calories: 638 | Fat: 42g | Carbs: 10g | Protein: 43g

Chicken Adobo

Prep Time: 10 minutes
Cooking Time: 40 minutes
Servings: 4
Ingredients:
4 chicken thighs
1/2 cup soy sauce
1/2 cup vinegar
4 cloves garlic, minced
2 bay leaves
1 teaspoon of peppercorns
1 onion, sliced

1 red chili (optional for heat)

Directions:
Combine soy sauce, vinegar, garlic, bay leaves, peppercorns, onion, and chili in the Ninja Foodi. Add chicken thighs and coat them in the mixture. Select the "Braise" function on low heat and cook for 30-40 minutes until the chicken is tender. Serve over steamed rice.

NUTRITION Calories: 384 | Fat: 22g | Carbs: 7g | Protein: 33g

Osso Buco (Braised Veal Shanks)

Prep Time: 20 minutes
Cooking Time: 1 hour 30 minutes
Servings: 4
Ingredients:
4 veal shanks
1/2 cup flour for dredging
2 tablespoons of olive oil
1 onion, chopped
2 carrots, chopped
2 celery stalks, chopped
4 cloves garlic, minced
1 cup white wine
2 cups beef or veal broth
2 tablespoons of tomato paste
2 sprigs thyme
Gremolata (zest of 1 lemon, 2 cloves minced garlic, 2 tablespoons of chopped parsley)

Directions:
Dredge veal shanks in flour.
Select the "Braise" function on high heat. Add olive oil and sear veal shanks until browned. Remove and set aside.
In the same Ninja cooker, add chopped onions, carrots, celery, and garlic. Sauté for 5 minutes until softened.
Stir in tomato paste and white wine.
Return the veal shanks to the pot, add broth and thyme.
Close the lid and set the Ninja Foodi to braise on low for 1 hour 30 minutes.
Serve the osso buco with gremolata over risotto or polenta.

NUTRITION Calories: 497 | Fat: 26g | Carbs: 15g | Protein: 39g

Pork Carnitas

Prep Time: 15 minutes
Cooking Time: 1 hour 30 minutes
Servings: 6
Ingredients:
3 lbs pork shoulder, cut into chunks
1 onion, chopped
4 cloves garlic, minced
1 teaspoon of cumin
1 teaspoon of oregano
1 teaspoon of chili powder
1/2 teaspoon of paprika
1/2 teaspoon of salt
1/4 teaspoon of black pepper
Juice of 2 oranges
Juice of 1 lime
1/2 cup chicken broth
2 bay leaves

Directions:
Combine pork, onion, garlic, spices, and citrus juices in the Ninja Foodi.
Select the "Braise" function on low heat and cook for 1 hour.
After an hour, add chicken broth and bay leaves. Continue to braise for another 30 minutes until the pork is tender.
Shred the pork using two forks and serve as tacos or burrito filling.

NUTRITION Calories: 497 | Fat: 36g | Carbs: 7g | Protein: 34g

Coq au Vin

Prep Time: 20 minutes
Cooking Time: 1 hour 30 minutes
Servings: 4
Ingredients:
4 chicken legs (thighs and drumsticks)
4 slices bacon, chopped
1 onion, chopped
2 carrots, chopped
2 cloves garlic, minced
1 cup red wine
1 cup chicken broth
1 tablespoon tomato paste
2 sprigs thyme
2 bay leaves
8 oz mushrooms, sliced
Salt and pepper to taste
Chopped parsley for garnish

Directions:

Select the "Braise" function on high heat. Add chopped bacon and cook until crisp. Remove and set aside.
In the Ninja cooker, add chicken pieces and sear until browned. Remove and set aside.
Add chopped onions, carrots, and garlic. Sauté for 5 minutes until softened.
Stir in tomato paste and red wine.
Return the chicken to the pot, add chicken broth, thyme, bay leaves, and season with salt and pepper.
Close the lid and set the Ninja Foodi to braise on low for 1 hour.
After an hour, add mushrooms and cook for an additional 30 minutes.
Garnish with chopped parsley before serving.

NUTRITION Calories: 519 | Fat: 23g | Carbs: 11g | Protein: 54g

Beef Stew

Prep Time: 20 minutes
Cooking Time: 1 hour 15 minutes
Servings: 6
Ingredients:
2 lbs beef stew meat, cubed
2 tablespoons of olive oil
1 onion, chopped
3 carrots, sliced
3 potatoes, diced
2 cloves garlic, minced
1 cup beef broth
1 cup red wine
1 can (14 oz) diced tomatoes
2 bay leaves
1 teaspoon of dried thyme
Salt and pepper to taste

Directions:
Select the "Braise" function on high heat. Add olive oil and sear the beef until browned. Remove and set aside.
In the same pot, add chopped onions, carrots, and garlic. Sauté for 5 minutes until softened.
Stir in red wine and simmer for 5 minutes to deglaze the pot.
Return the beef to the pot, add diced potatoes, diced tomatoes (with juices), beef broth, bay leaves, thyme, salt, and pepper.
Close the lid and set the Ninja Foodi to braise on low for 1 hour.
After an hour, check the stew for doneness and adjust seasoning if needed. Continue to braise for an additional 15 minutes if necessary.
Serve hot with crusty bread.

NUTRITION Calories: 460 | Fat: 18g | Carbs: 26g | Protein: 39g

Braised Chicken with Mushrooms

Prep Time: 15 minutes
Cooking Time: 1 hour
Servings: 4
Ingredients:
4 bone-in chicken thighs
8 oz mushrooms, sliced
1 onion, chopped
2 cloves garlic, minced
1 cup chicken broth
1/2 cup dry white wine
2 tablespoons of olive oil
2 sprigs fresh thyme
Salt and pepper to taste
Chopped fresh parsley for garnish

Directions:
Season the chicken thighs with salt and pepper.
Select the "Braise" function on high heat. Add olive oil and sear the chicken until browned. Remove and set aside.
In the same pot, add chopped onions and garlic. Sauté for 5 minutes until softened.
Add sliced mushrooms and sauté for another 5 minutes.
Pour in white wine and simmer for 5 minutes.
Return the chicken to the pot, add chicken broth, and fresh thyme.
Close the lid and set the Ninja Foodi to braise on low for 1 hour.
Garnish with chopped fresh parsley before serving.
NUTRITION Calories: 404 | Fat: 28g | Carbs: 7g | Protein: 30g

Red Wine Braised Beef

Prep Time: 20 minutes
Cooking Time: 2 hours
Servings: 6
Ingredients:
3 lbs beef chuck roast
2 tablespoons of olive oil
1 onion, chopped
2 carrots, chopped
3 cloves garlic, minced
2 cups red wine
1 cup beef broth
2 bay leaves
2 sprigs rosemary
Salt and pepper to taste

Directions:

Cut the beef into large chunks and sprinkle with salt and pepper.
Select the "Braise" function on high heat. Add olive oil and fry the beef until browned. Remove and let it rest.
In the same pot, add chopped onions, carrots, and garlic. Sauté for 5 minutes until softened.
Stir in red wine and simmer for 10 minutes to reduce.
Return the beef to the pot, add beef broth, bay leaves, and rosemary.
Close the lid and set the Ninja Foodi to braise on low for 2 hours.
Serve with mashed potatoes or polenta.
NUTRITION Calories: 485 | Fat: 34g | Carbs: 7g | Protein: 30g

Braised Pork Belly

Prep Time: 15 minutes
Cooking Time: 2 hours
Servings: 4
Ingredients:
2 lbs pork belly, cut into chunks
1 onion, chopped
3 cloves garlic, minced
1/2 cup soy sauce
1/2 cup mirin
1/4 cup brown sugar
1/4 cup water
2 star anise
1 cinnamon stick
2 bay leaves

Directions:
Select the "Braise" function on high heat. Add the pork belly chunks and sear until browned. Remove and set aside.
In the same pot, add chopped onions and garlic. Sauté for 5 minutes until softened.
Add soy sauce, mirin, brown sugar, water, star anise, cinnamon stick, and bay leaves. Stir to combine.
Return the pork belly to the pot.
Close the lid and set the Ninja Foodi to braise on low for 2 hours.
Serve the braised pork belly over rice or noodles.

NUTRITION Calories: 671 | Fat: 43g | Carbs: 15g | Protein: 22g

Braised Brussels Sprouts

Prep Time: 10 minutes
Cooking Time: 20 minutes
Servings: 4
Ingredients:
1 lb Brussels sprouts, trimmed and halved
2 tablespoons of olive oil
2 cloves garlic, minced
1/4 cup chicken or vegetable broth
2 tablespoons of balsamic vinegar
Salt and pepper to taste
Grated Parmesan cheese (optional, for garnish)

Directions:
Select the "Braise" function on high heat. Add olive oil and heat.
Add minced garlic and halved Brussels sprouts to the pot. Sauté for 5 minutes until they start to brown.
Pour in chicken or vegetable broth and balsamic vinegar. Stir to combine.
Close the lid and set the Ninja Foodi to braise on low for 15-20 minutes until the Brussels sprouts are tender.
Season with salt and pepper and garnish with grated Parmesan cheese if desired.

NUTRITION Calories:147 | Fat: 8g | Carbs: 16g | Protein: 5g

Beer-Braised Bratwurst

Prep Time: 10 minutes
Cooking Time: 30 minutes
Servings: 4
Ingredients:
4 bratwurst sausages
1 onion, sliced
2 cloves garlic, minced
12 oz beer (lager or ale)
1/2 cup chicken or beef broth
1 teaspoon of caraway seeds
4 hoagie rolls
Mustard and sauerkraut for serving

Directions:
Select the "Braise" function on medium heat. Add bratwurst sausages and brown them on all sides. Remove and set aside.
In the same pot, add sliced onions and minced garlic. Sauté for 5 minutes until softened.
Pour in beer and broth, and add caraway seeds.
Return the bratwurst sausages to the pot.
Close the lid and set the Ninja Foodi to braise on medium for 20-30 minutes until the sausages are cooked through.
Serve in hoagie rolls with mustard and sauerkraut.
NUTRITION Calories: 521 | Fat: 26g | Carbs: 41g | Protein: 23g

Moroccan Lamb Tagine

Prep Time: 15 minutes
Cooking Time: 1 hour 30 minutes
Servings: 4
Ingredients:
2 lbs boneless lamb shoulder, cubed
2 tablespoons of olive oil
1 onion, chopped
2 cloves garlic, minced
1 teaspoon of ground cumin
1 teaspoon of ground coriander
1 teaspoon of ground cinnamon
1/2 teaspoon of ground ginger
1/2 teaspoon of paprika
1/4 teaspoon of cayenne pepper (adjust to taste)
1 can (14 oz) diced tomatoes
1/2 cup dried apricots, chopped
1/4 cup almonds, toasted
Fresh cilantro for garnish
Cooked couscous or rice for serving

Directions:

Select the "Braise" function on high heat. Add olive oil and brown the lamb cubes. Remove and set aside.
In the same pot, add chopped onions and minced garlic. Sauté for 5 minutes until softened.
Stir in ground cumin, ground coriander, ground cinnamon, ground ginger, paprika, and cayenne pepper.
Add diced tomatoes, dried apricots, and toasted almonds. Mix well.
Return the lamb to the pot.
Close the lid and set the Ninja Foodi to braise on low for 1 hour 30 minutes.
Serve the Moroccan lamb tagine over cooked couscous or rice, garnished with fresh cilantro.

NUTRITION Calories: 585 | Fat: 33g | Carbs: 23g | Protein: 35g

Braised Duck Confit

Prep Time: 15 minutes
Cooking Time: 2 hours 30 minutes
Servings: 4
Ingredients:
4 duck leg quarters
2 teaspoon of kosher salt
1 teaspoon of black pepper
4 sprigs fresh thyme
4 cloves garlic, minced
2 cups duck fat (or substitute with olive oil)
Zest of 1 orange
1 bay leaf

Directions:
Season the duck leg quarters with kosher salt and black pepper.
Select the "Braise" function on low heat. Add duck fat (or olive oil) and heat.
Add minced garlic, fresh thyme, and bay leaf to the pot.
Place the duck leg quarters skin side down in the pot and cook for 1 hour on low.
Turn the duck leg quarters over, add orange zest, and continue to braise for an additional 1 hour.
Remove the duck confit from the pot and allow it to cool slightly.
If desired, crisp up the skin by placing the duck pieces under the broiler for a few minutes.
Serve with your choice of side dishes.

NUTRITION Calories: 778 | Fat: 56g | Carbs: 2g | Protein: 38g

Braised Rabbit with Mustard Sauce

Prep Time: 20 minutes
Cooking Time: 1 hour 30 minutes
Servings: 4
Ingredients:
1 whole rabbit, cut into pieces
2 tablespoons of olive oil
1 onion, chopped
2 cloves garlic, minced
1/4 cup Dijon mustard
1/4 cup white wine
1 cup chicken broth
2 sprigs fresh thyme
Salt and pepper to taste
Chopped fresh parsley for garnish

Directions:
Select the "Braise" function on high heat. Add olive oil and brown the rabbit pieces. Remove and set aside.

In the same pot, add chopped onions and minced garlic. Sauté for 5 minutes until softened.
Stir in Dijon mustard and white wine.
Return the rabbit to the pot, add chicken broth, fresh thyme, salt, and pepper.
Close the lid and set the Ninja Foodi to braise on low for 1 hour 30 minutes.
Garnish with chopped fresh parsley before serving.

NUTRITION Calories: 460 | Fat: 20g | Carbs: 4g | Protein: 51g

Braised Pork Chops with Apples

Prep Time: 15 minutes
Cooking Time: 1 hour
Servings: 4
Ingredients:
4 bone-in pork chops
2 tablespoons of butter
2 apples, sliced
1 onion, sliced
1/2 cup apple cider
1/2 cup chicken broth
2 sprigs fresh thyme
1 teaspoon of ground cinnamon
Salt and pepper to taste

Directions:
Season the pork chops with salt, pepper, and ground cinnamon.
Select the "Braise" function on medium heat. Add butter and sear the pork chops until browned. Remove and set aside.
In the same pot, add sliced apples and onions. Sauté for 5 minutes until they start to soften.
Pour in apple cider and chicken broth.
Return the pork chops to the pot, add fresh thyme, and cover with the apple-onion mixture.
Close the lid and set the Ninja Foodi to braise on low for 1 hour.
Serve with mashed potatoes or rice.

NUTRITION Calories: 529 | Fat: 34g | Carbs: 23g | Protein: 29g

Chinese Red-Braised Pork Belly

Prep Time: 15 minutes
Cooking Time: 1 hour 30 minutes
Servings: 4
Ingredients:
1 lb pork belly, cut into chunks
2 tablespoons of vegetable oil
2 cloves garlic, minced
1-inch piece fresh ginger, sliced
2 star anise
2 tablespoons of Shaoxing wine (or dry sherry)
2 tablespoons of soy sauce
1 tablespoon dark soy sauce
1 tablespoon brown sugar
1 cup water
Green onions for garnish
Steamed rice for serving

Directions:
Select the "Braise" function on high heat. Add vegetable oil and sear the pork belly until browned. Remove and set aside.
In the same pot, add minced garlic, sliced ginger, and star anise. Sauté for 2 minutes until fragrant.
Pour in Shaoxing wine, soy sauce, dark soy sauce, and brown sugar. Stir to combine.
Return the pork belly to the pot and add water.
Close the lid and set the Ninja Foodi to braise on low for 1 hour 30 minutes.
Serve with steamed rice, garnished with chopped green onions.

NUTRITION Calories: 552 | Fat: 51g | Carbs: 7g | Protein: 16g

Braised Beef and Noodles

Prep Time: 15 minutes
Cooking Time: 1 hour 30 minutes
Servings: 4
Ingredients:
1 lb beef stew meat, cubed
2 tablespoons of vegetable oil
1 onion, chopped
2 carrots, chopped
2 cloves garlic, minced
2 cups beef broth
1/4 cup soy sauce
1 teaspoon of Chinese five-spice powder
8 oz egg noodles
Green onions for garnish

Directions:

Select the "Braise" function on high heat. Add vegetable oil and sear the beef cubes until browned. Remove and set aside.
In the same pot, add chopped onions, carrots, and minced garlic. Sauté for 5 minutes until softened.
Stir in beef broth, soy sauce, and Chinese five-spice powder.
Return the beef to the pot and close the lid. Set the Ninja Foodi to braise on low for 1 hour 30 minutes.
While the beef is braising, cook the egg noodles according to package instructions.
Serve the braised beef over cooked egg noodles, garnished with chopped green onions.

NUTRITION Calories: 585 | Fat: 21g | Carbs: 65g | Protein: 37g

Italian Braised Chicken Thighs

Prep Time: 15 minutes
Cooking Time: 1 hour 30 minutes
Servings: 4
Ingredients:
4 bone-in chicken thighs
2 tablespoons of olive oil
1 onion, chopped
2 cloves garlic, minced
1 can (14 oz) crushed tomatoes
1/2 cup dry white wine
1/2 cup chicken broth
1 teaspoon of dried oregano
1 teaspoon of dried basil
1/2 teaspoon of red pepper flakes (adjust to taste)
Salt and pepper to taste
Fresh basil leaves for garnish
Grated Parmesan cheese for serving

Directions:
Season the chicken thighs with salt, pepper, dried oregano, and dried basil.
Select the "Braise" function on high heat. Add olive oil and sear the chicken thighs until browned. Remove and set aside.
In the same pot, add chopped onions and minced garlic. Sauté for 5 minutes until softened.
Stir in crushed tomatoes, white wine, chicken broth, and red pepper flakes.
Return the chicken to the pot and close the lid. Set the Ninja Foodi to braise on low for 1 hour 30 minutes.
Serve with fresh basil leaves and grated Parmesan cheese.

NUTRITION Calories: 425 | Fat: 24g | Carbs: 11g | Protein: 35g

Braised Kale with Garlic and Lemon

Prep Time: 10 minutes
Cooking Time: 20 minutes
Servings: 4
Ingredients:
1 bunch kale, stems removed and leaves chopped
2 tablespoons of olive oil
3 cloves garlic, minced
Zest and juice of 1 lemon
1/4 cup chicken or vegetable broth
Salt and pepper to taste
Grated Parmesan cheese for serving (optional)

Directions:
Select the "Braise" function on medium heat. Add olive oil and minced garlic. Sauté for 1 minute until fragrant. Add chopped kale to the pot and sauté for 3-4 minutes until it begins to wilt.
Pour in chicken or vegetable broth, lemon zest, and lemon juice. Stir to combine.
Close the lid and set the Ninja Foodi to braise on low for 15-20 minutes until the kale is tender.
Season with salt and pepper and serve with grated Parmesan cheese if desired.

NUTRITION Calories: 107 | **Fat:** 7g | **Carbs:** 11g | **Protein:** 3g

Braised Tofu with Ginger and Scallions

Prep Time: 15 minutes
Cooking Time: 30 minutes
Servings: 4
Ingredients:
1 block (14 oz) extra-firm tofu, cubed
2 tablespoons of vegetable oil
2 cloves garlic, minced
1-inch piece fresh ginger, sliced
3 scallions, sliced
2 tablespoons of soy sauce
1 tablespoon hoisin sauce
1 cup vegetable broth
1 teaspoon of cornstarch
Salt and pepper to taste
Steamed rice for serving

Directions:
Select the "Braise" function on medium heat. Add vegetable oil and cubed tofu. Sauté until the tofu is lightly browned. Remove and set aside.

In the same pot, add minced garlic, sliced ginger, and sliced scallions. Sauté for 2 minutes until fragrant.
Stir in soy sauce, hoisin sauce, and vegetable broth. Return the tofu to the pot.
In a small bowl, mix cornstarch with a little water to make a slurry. Stir it into the pot to thicken the sauce.
Close the lid and set the Ninja Foodi to braise on medium for 15-20 minutes. Serve over steamed rice.

NUTRITION Calories: 226 | **Fat:** 16g | **Carbs:** 10g | **Protein:** 14g

Braised Fennel with Parmesan

Prep Time: 10 minutes
Cooking Time: 25 minutes
Servings: 4
Ingredients:
2 bulbs fennel, trimmed and sliced
2 tablespoons of olive oil
2 cloves garlic, minced
1/4 cup chicken or vegetable broth
1/4 cup grated Parmesan cheese
Salt and pepper to taste
Fresh chopped parsley for garnish

Directions:
Select the "Braise" function on medium heat. Add olive oil and sliced fennel. Sauté for 5 minutes until lightly browned.
Add minced garlic and continue to sauté for another 2 minutes until fragrant.
Pour in chicken or vegetable broth and stir.
Close the lid and set the Ninja Foodi to braise on medium for 15-20 minutes until the fennel is tender.
Season with salt and pepper and garnish with grated Parmesan cheese and fresh chopped parsley.

NUTRITION Calories: 103 | **Fat:** 7g | **Carbs:** 9g | **Protein:** 4g

Braised Artichokes with Lemon and Garlic

Prep Time: 15 minutes
Cooking Time: 30 minutes
Servings: 4
Ingredients:
4 whole artichokes, trimmed and halved
2 tablespoons of olive oil
4 cloves garlic, minced
Zest and juice of 1 lemon
1/4 cup chicken or vegetable broth
Salt and pepper to taste

Directions:
Select the "Braise" function on medium heat. Add olive oil and halved artichokes. Sauté for 5 mins until they start to brown.
Add garlic and sauté for 2 mins until fragrant.
Pour in chicken or vegetable broth, lemon zest, and lemon juice.
Close the lid and set the Ninja Foodi to braise on medium for 20-25 minutes until the artichokes are tender.
Sprinkle with salt and pepper before serving.
NUTRITION Calories: 101 | Fat: 7g | Carbs: 10g | Protein: 3g

Coconut Braised Chickpeas

Prep Time: 10 minutes
Cooking Time: 25 minutes
Servings: 4
Ingredients:
2 cans (15 oz each) chickpeas, drained and rinsed
1 can (14 oz) coconut milk
1 onion, chopped
2 cloves garlic, minced
1 teaspoon of ground cumin
1 teaspoon of ground coriander
1/2 teaspoon of ground turmeric
1/2 teaspoon of ground paprika
1/2 teaspoon of cayenne pepper (adjust to taste)
Salt and pepper to taste
Chopped fresh cilantro for garnish
Cooked rice for serving

Directions:
Select the "Braise" function on medium heat. Add chopped onions and minced garlic. Sauté for 5 minutes until softened.
Stir in ground cumin, ground coriander, ground turmeric, ground paprika, and cayenne pepper.

Add drained chickpeas and coconut milk. Mix well.
Close the lid and set the Ninja Foodi to braise on medium for 20-25 minutes.
Season with salt and pepper and garnish with chopped fresh cilantro.
Serve over cooked rice.

NUTRITION Calories: 418 | Fat: 19g | Carbs: 51g | Protein: 15g

Braised Green Beans with Tomatoes

Prep Time: 10 minutes
Cooking Time: 20 minutes
Servings: 4
Ingredients:
1 lb green beans, trimmed
2 tablespoons of olive oil
1 onion, chopped
2 cloves garlic, minced
1 can (14 oz) diced tomatoes
1 teaspoon of dried oregano
Salt and pepper to taste

Directions:
Select the "Braise" function on medium heat. Add olive oil and chopped onions. Sauté for 5 mins until softened.
Add garlic and sauté for 2 mins until fragrant.
Add tomatoes (with juices) and oregano. Add trimmed green beans and mix well.
Close the lid and set the Ninja Foodi to braise on medium for 15-20 mins until the green beans are tender.
Sprinkle with salt and pepper before serving.

NUTRITION Calories: 103 | Fat: 7g | Carbs: 9g | Protein: 2g

Braised Cabbage with Bacon

Prep Time: 15 minutes
Cooking Time: 30 minutes
Servings: 4
Ingredients:
1 small head of cabbage, shredded
4 slices bacon, chopped
1 onion, chopped
2 cloves garlic, minced
1/2 cup chicken or vegetable broth
Salt and pepper to taste
Chopped fresh parsley for garnish

Directions:
Select the "Braise" function on medium heat. Add chopped bacon and cook until crisp. Remove and set aside.
In the same pot, add chopped onions and minced garlic. Sauté for 5 minutes until softened.
Stir in shredded cabbage and sauté for another 5 minutes.
Pour in chicken or vegetable broth.
Close the lid and set the Ninja Foodi to braise on medium for 20-25 minutes until the cabbage is tender.
Sprinkle with salt and pepper, and garnish with chopped fresh parsley.

NUTRITION Calories: 139 | Fat: 8g | Carbs: 16g | Protein: 5g

Thai Massaman Curry

Prep Time: 15 minutes
Cooking Time: 40 minutes
Servings: 4
Ingredients:
1 lb boneless chicken thighs, cut into chunks
1 can (14 oz) coconut milk
2 tablespoons of Massaman curry paste
2 potatoes, diced
1 onion, chopped
2 cloves garlic, minced
1/2 cup chicken broth
1/4 cup roasted peanuts
2 tablespoons of fish sauce
1 tablespoon brown sugar
1 tablespoon tamarind paste
1 cinnamon stick
2 cardamom pods
2 bay leaves
Salt and pepper to taste
Cooked rice for serving

Directions:
Select the "Braise" function on medium heat. Add chicken chunks and brown them. Remove and set aside.

In the same pot, add chopped onions and minced garlic. Sauté for 5 minutes until softened.
Stir in Massaman curry paste and cook for 2 minutes until fragrant.
Add diced potatoes, chicken broth, coconut milk, roasted peanuts, fish sauce, brown sugar, tamarind paste, cinnamon stick, cardamom pods, and bay leaves. Return the chicken to the pot.
Close the lid and set the Ninja Foodi to braise on medium for 30-40 minutes until the potatoes are tender.
Sprinkle with salt and pepper before serving with cooked rice.

NUTRITION Calories: 539 | Fat: 34g | Carbs: 29g | Protein: 26g

Braised Sweet Potatoes with Maple Glaze

Prep Time: 10 minutes
Cooking Time: 30 minutes
Servings: 4
Ingredients:
4 sweet potatoes, peeled and cubed
2 tablespoons of butter
1/4 cup maple syrup
1/4 cup chicken or vegetable broth
1/2 teaspoon of ground cinnamon
1/4 teaspoon of ground nutmeg
Salt and pepper to taste
Chopped fresh parsley for garnish

Directions:
Select the "Braise" function on medium heat. Add butter and melt.
Add cubed sweet potatoes and sauté for 5 minutes until they start to brown.
Pour in maple syrup, chicken or vegetable broth, ground cinnamon, and ground nutmeg.
Close the lid and set the Ninja Foodi to braise on medium for 25-30 minutes until the sweet potatoes are tender.
Sprinkle with salt and pepper and garnish with chopped fresh parsley.

NUTRITION Calories: 274 | Fat: 6g | Carbs: 54g | Protein: 3g

CHAPTER SEVEN

STEAM RECIPES

Steamed Asparagus with Lemon Butter

Prep Time: 5 minutes
Cooking Time: 5 minutes
Servings: 4
Ingredients:
1 bunch of fresh asparagus
2 tablespoons of unsalted butter
1 lemon, zested and juiced
Salt and black pepper to taste

Directions:
Trim the tough ends of the asparagus spears.
Place the asparagus in the Ninja Foodi's steamer basket.
Pour 1 cup of water into the inner Ninja Foodi pot and insert the Ninja steamer basket.
Close the lid, select the "Steam" function, and set the timer to 5 minutes.
While the asparagus is steaming, melt the butter in a small saucepan. Stir in the lemon zest and juice. Season with salt and pepper.
Once the asparagus is tender, remove it from the steamer basket and drizzle the lemon butter sauce over it. Serve immediately.
NUTRITION Calories: 77 | Fat: 6g | Carbs: 5g | Protein: 2g

Steamed Salmon with Dill Sauce

Prep Time: 10 minutes
Cooking Time: 10 minutes
Servings: 2
Ingredients:
2 salmon fillets
Salt and black pepper to taste
1 tablespoon olive oil
1 lemon, thinly sliced
For the Dill Sauce:
1/2 cup plain Greek yogurt
1 tablespoon fresh dill, chopped
1 teaspoon of lemon juice
Salt and black pepper to taste

Directions:
Season the salmon fillets with salt and pepper.
Place a trivet or a steamer rack in the Ninja Foodi inner pot.
Add 1 cup of water to the inner pot and set the salmon fillets on the trivet or rack. Drizzle with olive oil and top with lemon slices.
Close the lid, select the "Steam" function, and set the timer to 10 minutes.
While the salmon is steaming, prepare the dill sauce by mixing together all the sauce ingredients in a bowl.
Once the salmon is cooked, serve it with the dill sauce on the side.
NUTRITION Calories: 332 | Fat: 20g | Carbs: 4g | Protein: 33g

Steamed Broccoli with Garlic Butter

Prep Time: 5 minutes
Cooking Time: 5 minutes
Servings: 4
Ingredients:
1 head of broccoli, cut into florets
2 tablespoons of unsalted butter
2 cloves garlic, minced
Salt and black pepper to taste

Directions:
Place the broccoli florets in the Ninja Foodi's steamer basket.
Add 1 cup of water to the inner pot and insert the steamer basket.
Close the lid, select the "Steam" function, and set the timer to 5 minutes.
While the broccoli is steaming, melt the butter in a small saucepan. Add the minced garlic and sauté for a minute or until fragrant. Season with salt and pepper.
Once the broccoli is tender, remove it from the steamer basket and drizzle the garlic butter sauce over it. Serve immediately.
NUTRITION Calories: 82 | Fat: 6g | Carbs: 7g | Protein: 3g

Steamed Artichokes with Lemon Garlic Aioli

Prep Time: 10 minutes
Cooking Time: 20 minutes
Servings: 2
Ingredients:
2 large artichokes
1 lemon, halved
2 cloves garlic, minced
1/2 cup mayonnaise
1 teaspoon of lemon juice
Salt and black pepper to taste

Directions:
Trim the tops and stems of the artichokes. Cut off any sharp thorns from the leaves.
Squeeze the lemon halves over the cut parts of the artichokes to prevent browning.
Place a trivet or steamer rack in the Ninja Foodi inner pot. Add 1 cup of water.
Set the artichokes on the trivet or rack. Close the lid, select the "Steam" function, and set the timer to 20 minutes.
While the artichokes are steaming, prepare the lemon garlic aioli by mixing together minced garlic, mayonnaise, lemon juice, salt, and pepper in a bowl.
Once the artichokes are tender (you can easily pull off a leaf), serve them with the lemon garlic aioli for dipping.
NUTRITION Calories: 368 | Fat: 31g | Carbs: 20g | Protein: 7g

Steamed Rice with Vegetables

Prep Time: 10 minutes
Cooking Time: 15 minutes
Servings: 4
Ingredients:
1 cup white rice
2 cups water
1 cup mixed vegetables (carrots, peas, corn)
Salt and black pepper to taste

Directions:
Rinse the rice thoroughly until the water runs clear.
In the Ninja Foodi inner pot, combine the rinsed rice, water, mixed vegetables, salt, and pepper.
Close the lid, select the "Steam" function, and set the timer to 15 minutes.
Serve and enjoy.

NUTRITION Calories: 203 | Fat: 1g | Carbs: 44g | Protein: 4g

Steamed Mussels in White Wine

Prep Time: 15 minutes
Cooking Time: 10 minutes
Servings: 2
Ingredients:
2 pounds fresh mussels, cleaned and debearded
1 cup dry white wine
2 cloves garlic, minced
2 tablespoons of butter
2 tablespoons of fresh parsley, chopped
Salt and black pepper to taste

Directions:
In the Ninja Foodi inner pot, combine the white wine and minced garlic.
Place the cleaned mussels in the steamer basket and set it in the inner pot.
Close the lid, select the "Steam" function, and set the timer to 10 minutes.
While the mussels are steaming, melt the butter in a saucepan and stir in half of the chopped parsley.
Once the mussels have opened (discard any that don't), transfer them to a serving dish, pour the garlic butter sauce over them, and garnish with the remaining parsley. Sprinkle with salt and pepper.
Serve with crusty bread to soak up the delicious broth.
NUTRITION Calories: 350 | Fat: 13g | Carbs: 15g | Protein: 32g

Steamed Dumplings (Potstickers)

Prep Time: 20 minutes
Cooking Time: 10 minutes
Servings: 4
Ingredients:
20 dumplings (frozen or homemade)
1/4 cup soy sauce
2 tablespoons of rice vinegar
1 tablespoon sesame oil
1 green onion, chopped

Directions:
Place a trivet or steamer rack in the Ninja Foodi inner pot and add 1 cup of water.
Arrange the dumplings on the trivet or in a steamer basket.
Close the lid, select the "Steam" function, and set the timer to 10 minutes.
While the dumplings are steaming, prepare the dipping sauce by mixing soy sauce, rice vinegar, sesame oil, and chopped green onion in a bowl.
Once the dumplings are cooked, serve them with the dipping sauce.
NUTRITION Calories: 222 | Fat: 5g | Carbs: 36g | Protein: 7g

Steamed Lemon Herb Chicken

Prep Time: 15 minutes
Cooking Time: 15 minutes
Servings: 4
Ingredients:
4 boneless, skinless chicken breasts
1 lemon, thinly sliced
2 cloves garlic, minced
2 tablespoons of fresh thyme, chopped
Salt and black pepper to taste

Directions:
Season the chicken breasts with minced garlic, chopped thyme, salt, and pepper.
Place a trivet or steamer rack in the Ninja Foodi inner pot.
Set the chicken breasts on the trivet and top with lemon slices.
Close the lid, select the "Steam" function, and set the timer to 15 minutes.
Once the chicken is cooked through, serve it with steamed vegetables or a side salad.
NUTRITION Calories: 172 | Fat: 3g | Carbs: 5g | Protein: 29g

Steamed Lobster Tails

Prep Time: 10 minutes
Cooking Time: 8 minutes
Servings: 2
Ingredients:
2 lobster tails
2 tablespoons of melted butter
1 lemon, cut into wedges
Fresh parsley for garnish
Salt and black pepper to taste

Directions:
Using kitchen shears, cut the top of the lobster shells lengthwise.
Place a trivet or steamer rack in the Ninja Foodi inner pot and add 1 cup of water.
Arrange the lobster tails on the trivet.
Close the lid, select the "Steam" function, and set the timer to 8 minutes.
While the lobster tails are steaming, melt the butter and prepare lemon wedges.
Once the lobster tails are cooked, serve them with melted butter, lemon wedges, and garnish with fresh parsley. Season with salt and pepper.
NUTRITION Calories: 187 | Fat: 6g | Carbs: 2g | Protein: 31g

Steamed Tofu with Ginger Sesame Sauce

Prep Time: 15 minutes
Cooking Time: 10 minutes
Servings: 4
Ingredients:
1 block of firm tofu, cubed
2 tablespoons of soy sauce
1 tablespoon sesame oil
1 tablespoon rice vinegar
1 teaspoon of fresh ginger, minced
1 teaspoon of honey
1 green onion, thinly sliced
Sesame seeds for garnish

Directions:
Place the tofu cubes in the Ninja Foodi's steamer basket.
In a small bowl, combine soy sauce, sesame oil, rice vinegar, ginger, and honey to create the sauce.
Add 1 cup of water to the inner pot and insert the steamer basket with tofu.
Close the lid, select the "Steam" function, and set the timer to 10 minutes.
Once the tofu is heated through and tender, transfer it to a serving plate, drizzle with the sauce, and garnish with sliced green onions and sesame seeds.
NUTRITION Calories: 118 | Fat: 9g | Carbs: 4g | Protein: 7g

Steamed Vegetable Medley with Herb Butter

Prep Time: 10 minutes
Cooking Time: 10 minutes
Servings: 4
Ingredients:
2 cups mixed vegetables (carrots, broccoli, cauliflower) 2 tablespoons of unsalted butter
1 tablespoon fresh herbs (e.g., thyme, rosemary), chopped
Salt and black pepper to taste

Directions:
Place the mixed vegetables in the Ninja Foodi's steamer basket. Pour 1 cup of water into the inner Ninja Foodi pot and insert the Ninja steamer basket. Close the lid, select the "Steam" function, and set the timer to 10 minutes. While the vegetables are steaming, melt the butter in a small saucepan. Stir in the fresh herbs and season with salt and pepper.
Once the vegetables are tender, remove them from the steamer basket and drizzle the herb butter sauce over them. Serve as a side dish.
NUTRITION Calories: 95 | Fat: 7g | Carbs:9g | Protein: 2g

Steamed Clams in White Wine and Garlic

Prep Time: 15 minutes
Cooking Time: 10 minutes
Servings: 2
Ingredients:
2 pounds fresh clams, cleaned
1 cup dry white wine
4 cloves garlic, minced
2 tablespoons of butter
2 tablespoons of fresh parsley, chopped
Salt and black pepper to taste
Crusty bread for dipping

Directions:
In the Ninja Foodi inner pot, combine the white wine and minced garlic.
Place the cleaned clams in the steamer basket and set it in the inner pot.
Close the lid, select the "Steam" function, and set the timer to 10 minutes.
While the clams are steaming, melt the butter in a saucepan and stir in half of the chopped parsley. Season with salt and pepper.
Once the clams have opened (discard any that don't), transfer them to a serving dish, pour the garlic butter sauce over them, and garnish with the remaining parsley. Serve with crusty bread for dipping.

NUTRITION Calories: 308 | Fat: 10g | Carbs: 12g | Protein: 38g

Steamed Cod with Lemon Butter Sauce

Prep Time: 15 minutes
Cooking Time: 12 minutes
Servings: 2
Ingredients:
2 cod fillets
Salt and black pepper to taste
2 tablespoons of unsalted butter
1 lemon, juiced and zested
2 cloves garlic, minced
Fresh parsley for garnish

Directions:
Season the cod fillets with salt and pepper.
Place a trivet or steamer rack in the Ninja Foodi inner pot. Set the cod fillets on the trivet.
Close the lid, select the "Steam" function, and set the timer to 12 minutes.
While the cod is steaming, melt the butter in a small saucepan. Add minced garlic, lemon juice, and zest. Season with salt and pepper.

Once the cod is cooked and flakes easily, transfer it to serving plates, drizzle with the lemon butter sauce, and garnish with fresh parsley.

NUTRITION Calories: 355 | Fat: 17g | Carbs: 3g | Protein: 48g

Steamed Jasmine Rice with Coconut Milk

Prep Time: 5 minutes
Cooking Time: 15 minutes
Servings: 4
Ingredients:
1 cup jasmine rice
1 cup coconut milk
1 cup water
1/2 teaspoon of salt
Fresh cilantro for garnish (optional)

Directions:
Rinse the rice properly.
In the Ninja Foodi inner pot, combine the rice, water, coconut milk, and salt.
Close the lid, select the "Steam" function, and set the timer to 15 minutes.
Once the rice is done, garnish with fresh cilantro if desired and serve as a side dish.

NUTRITION Calories: 336 | Fat: 14g | Carbs: 49g | Protein: 6g

Steamed Shrimp with Old Bay Seasoning

Prep Time: 10 minutes
Cooking Time: 5 minutes
Servings: 4
Ingredients:
1 pound large shrimp, peeled and deveined
2 tablespoons of Old Bay seasoning
Lemon wedges for serving

Directions:
Toss the peeled and deveined shrimp with Old Bay seasoning.
Place a trivet or steamer rack in the Ninja Foodi inner pot. Arrange the seasoned shrimp on the trivet.
Close the lid, select the "Steam" function, and set the timer to 5 minutes.
Once the shrimp turn pink and are cooked through, serve them with lemon wedges.

NUTRITION Calories: 117 | Fat: 1g | Carbs: 1g | Protein: 23g

Steamed Veggie and Tofu Stir-Fry

Prep Time: 15 minutes
Cooking Time: 10 minutes
Servings: 4
Ingredients:
1 block of firm tofu, cubed
2 cups mixed vegetables (broccoli, bell peppers, snap peas)
2 tablespoons of soy sauce
1 tablespoon sesame oil
1 teaspoon of fresh ginger, minced
2 cloves garlic, minced
Salt and black pepper to taste
Cooked rice for serving

Directions:
Place the cubed tofu and mixed vegetables in the Ninja Foodi's steamer basket.
In a small bowl, combine soy sauce, sesame oil, ginger, garlic, salt, and pepper.
Pour 1 cup of water into the inner Ninja Foodi pot and insert the Ninja steamer basket.
Close the lid, select the "Steam" function, and set the timer to 10 minutes.
While the tofu and vegetables are steaming, prepare cooked rice.
Once the tofu and vegetables are tender, serve them over the cooked rice and drizzle with the soy sauce mixture.
NUTRITION Calories: 194 | Fat: 10g | Carbs: 13g | Protein: 16g

Steamed Lemon Pudding Cakes

Prep Time: 15 minutes
Cooking Time: 25 minutes
Servings: 4
Ingredients:
1/2 cup granulated sugar
2 tablespoons of unsalted butter, softened
2 large eggs, separated
2 tablespoons of all-purpose flour
1 lemon, zest and juice
1 cup milk
Powdered sugar for dusting

Directions:
In a mixing bowl, cream together sugar and softened butter.
Beat in the egg yolks one at a time.
Stir in the flour, lemon zest, and lemon juice.
Gradually add the milk and mix until smooth.

In another clean bowl, whisk the egg whites.
Carefully pour the egg whites into the lemon mixture.
Pour the batter into four greased ramekins.
Place the ramekins on the Ninja Foodi's steamer rack.
Close the lid, select the "Steam" function, and set the timer to 25 minutes.
Once the pudding cakes are set and lightly golden, remove them from the Ninja Foodi.
Dust with powdered sugar before serving. They're best served warm.
NUTRITION Calories: 265 | Fat: 10g | Carbs: 39g | Protein: 6g

Steamed Thai Green Curry with Tofu

Prep Time: 15 minutes
Cooking Time: 15 minutes
Servings: 4
Ingredients:
1 block of firm tofu, cubed
1 can (14 oz) coconut milk
2 tablespoons of green curry paste
2 cups mixed vegetables (e.g., bell peppers, zucchini, carrots)
2 tablespoons of fish sauce (for non-vegetarian version)
1 tablespoon brown sugar
Fresh basil leaves for garnish
Cooked jasmine rice for serving

Directions:
In a bowl, mix the green curry paste, coconut milk, fish sauce (if using), and brown sugar until well combined.
Place the cubed tofu and mixed vegetables in the Ninja Foodi's steamer basket.
Pour the curry mixture over the tofu and vegetables.
Close the lid, select the "Steam" function, and set the timer to 15 minutes.
While the curry is steaming, prepare jasmine rice.
Once the vegetables are tender and the curry is fragrant, serve it over jasmine rice and garnish with fresh basil leaves.
NUTRITION Calories: 283 | Fat: 21g | Carbs: 20g | Protein: 8g

Steamed Lemon and Herb Asparagus

Prep Time: 10 minutes
Cooking Time: 5 minutes
Servings: 4
Ingredients:
1 bunch of fresh asparagus
2 tablespoons of olive oil
1 lemon, zested and juiced
2 cloves garlic, minced
1 tablespoon fresh herbs (e.g., thyme, rosemary), chopped
Salt and black pepper to taste

Directions:
Trim the tough ends of the asparagus spears.
Place the asparagus in the Ninja Foodi's steamer basket.
In a clean bowl, combine herbs, salt, olive oil, lemon zest, garlic, lemon juice, and pepper. Drizzle the lemon herb mixture over the asparagus. Close the lid, select the "Steam" function, and set the timer to 5 minutes.
Once the asparagus is tender-crisp and has absorbed the flavors, serve immediately.
NUTRITION Calories: 80 | Fat: 7g | Carbs: 5g | Protein: 3g

Steamed Pumpkin Custard

Prep Time: 15 minutes
Cooking Time: 25 minutes
Servings: 4
Ingredients:
1 cup pumpkin puree (canned or homemade)
2 eggs
1/2 cup coconut milk
1/4 cup granulated sugar
1/2 teaspoon of ground cinnamon
1/4 teaspoon of ground nutmeg
1/4 teaspoon of vanilla extract
Whipped cream for garnish (optional)

Directions:

In a mixing bowl, combine pumpkin puree, eggs, coconut milk, sugar, cinnamon, nutmeg, and vanilla extract until smooth.
Pour the mixture into four greased ramekins.
Place the ramekins on the Ninja Foodi's steamer rack.
Close the lid, select the "Steam" function, and set the timer to 25 minutes.
Once the pumpkin custards are set and slightly firm, remove them from the Ninja Foodi.
Allow them to cool slightly, then garnish with whipped cream if desired before serving.
NUTRITION Calories: 223 | Fat: 10g | Carbs: 9g | Protein: 11g

Steamed Lemon Garlic Shrimp Pasta

Prep Time: 20 minutes
Cooking Time: 15 minutes
Servings: 4
Ingredients:
8 oz linguine or spaghetti
1 pound large shrimp, peeled and deveined
2 tablespoons of olive oil
4 cloves garlic, minced
Zest and juice of 1 lemon
1/4 cup fresh parsley, chopped
Salt and black pepper to taste
Grated Parmesan cheese for garnish

Directions:
Cook the spaghetti according to package cooking method. Drain and set aside.
In a clean bowl, toss the shrimp with olive oil, minced garlic, lemon zest, lemon juice, fresh parsley, salt, and black pepper.
Place the seasoned shrimp in the Ninja Foodi's steamer basket.
Close the lid, select the "Steam" function, and set the timer to 15 minutes.
While the shrimp are steaming, reheat the cooked pasta.
Once the shrimp are pink and cooked through, serve them over the hot pasta and garnish with grated Parmesan cheese.

NUTRITION Calories: 546 | Fat: 21g | Carbs: 54g | Protein: 34g

CHAPTER EIGHT
SOUS VIDE RECIPES

Sous Vide Steak

Prep Time: 10 minutes
Cooking Time: 1-4 hours (sous vide), 5 minutes (searing)
Serving: 2
Ingredients:
2 sirloin or ribeye steaks (1 inch thick)
Salt and pepper to taste
2 sprigs of fresh rosemary (optional)
2 cloves of garlic, crushed (optional)
Olive oil (for searing)

Directions:
Fill the Ninja Foodi possible cooker pro with water according to the manufacturer's instructions. Preheat the sous vide function to your desired steak temperature (e.g., 130°F for medium-rare).
Season the steaks generously with salt and pepper. Place each steak in a separate sous vide bag, adding a sprig of rosemary and a crushed garlic clove to each bag if desired.
Seal the sous vide bags, ensuring they're airtight to prevent water from entering.
Place the sealed bags in the preheated Ninja Foodi sous vide water bath. Cook for 1 to 4 hours, depending on your preferred steak doneness.
After sous vide cooking, remove the steaks from the bags and pat them dry with paper towels.
Preheat a skillet over high heat with a bit of olive oil. Sear the steaks for about 1-2 minutes on each side until a golden crust forms.
Allow the steaks to rest for a few minutes before slicing. Serve hot and enjoy your perfectly sous vide cooked steak.
NUTRITION Calories: 560 | Fat: 42g | Carbs: 2g | Protein: 47g

Sous Vide Salmon

Prep Time: 10 minutes
Cooking Time: 45 minutes
Serving: 2
Ingredients:
2 salmon fillets
Salt and pepper to taste
Fresh dill or lemon slices for garnish (optional)

Directions:

Fill the Ninja Foodi possible cooker pro with water according to the manufacturer's instructions. Preheat the sous vide function to 130°F (54°C).
Season the salmon fillets with salt and pepper and place them in a sous vide bag.
Seal the bag and submerge it in the preheated water. Cook for 45 minutes.
Carefully remove the salmon from the bag and gently pat dry. Sear briefly in a hot skillet for a nice crust.
Garnish with fresh dill or lemon slices and serve immediately.
NUTRITION Calories: 350 | Fat: 18g | Carbs: 7g | Protein: 33g

Sous Vide Chicken Breast

Prep Time: 10 minutes
Cooking Time: 1-4 hours
Serving: 2
Ingredients:
2 boneless, skinless chicken breasts
Salt, pepper, and your choice of seasoning
Olive oil for searing

Directions:
Fill the Ninja Foodi possible cooker pro with water and preheat to 140°F (60°C) using the "sous vide" function.
Season the chicken breasts with salt, pepper, and your preferred seasoning.
Place the chicken breasts in sous vide bags and seal. Submerge the bags in the preheated water and cook for 1-4 hours.
Remove chicken from the bags and pat dry. Sear in a hot skillet with olive oil for a minute on each side.
Slice and serve with your favorite sides.

NUTRITION Calories: 342 | Fat: 23g | Carbs: 8g | Protein: 41g

Sous Vide Pork Tenderloin

Prep Time: 10 minutes
Cooking Time: 2-4 hours
Serving: 4
Ingredients:
1 pork tenderloin
Salt, pepper, and your choice of herbs/spices
Olive oil for searing

Directions:
Fill the Ninja Foodi possible cooker pro with water and preheat to 140°F (60°C) using the "sous vide" function.
Season the pork tenderloin with salt, pepper, and your desired herbs/spices.
Place the seasoned pork tenderloin in a sous vide bag, seal, and submerge in the preheated water. Cook for 2-4 hours.
Remove the pork tenderloin from the bag and pat dry. Sear in a hot skillet with olive oil for a minute on each side.
Slice and serve with your choice of sides.

NUTRITION Calories: 360 | Fat: 20g | Carbs: 5g | Protein: 43g

Sous Vide Garlic Confit

Prep Time: 10 minutes
Cooking Time: 2-4 hours
Serving: Varies
Ingredients:
Whole garlic bulbs, halved horizontally
Olive oil
Salt
Fresh herbs (optional)

Directions:
Fill the Ninja Foodi possible cooker pro with water and preheat to 185°F (85°C) using the "sous vide" function.
Place halved garlic bulbs in a sous vide bag. Add a drizzle of olive oil, a sprinkle of salt, and fresh herbs if using.
Seal the bag and submerge in the preheated water. Cook for 2-4 hours.
Remove the garlic from the bag and use it in various dishes like spreads, pastas, or as a flavorful addition to your favorite recipes.

NUTRITION Calories: 120 | Fat: 9g | Carbs: 3g | Protein: 1g

Sous Vide Pork Belly

Prep Time: 15 minutes
Cooking Time: 12-24 hours Serving: 4-6
Ingredients:
1 lb (450g) pork belly, skin on
Salt and pepper
1 tbsp soy sauce
1 tbsp brown sugar
1 tsp five-spice powder

Directions:
Fill the Ninja Foodi possible cooker pro and preheat to 155°F (68°C) using the "sous vide" function.
Season the pork belly with salt and pepper. Place it in a sous vide bag with soy sauce, brown sugar, and five-spice powder.
Seal the bag and submerge in the preheated water. Cook for 12-24 hours.
Remove the pork belly from the bag and pat dry. Sear in a hot skillet or under a broiler until crispy.
Slice and serve with your favorite accompaniments.

NUTRITION Calories: 422 | Fat: 39g | Carbs: 4g | Protein: 14g

Sous Vide Creme Brulee

Prep Time: 15 minutes
Cooking Time: 1-2 hours Serving: 4
Ingredients:
2 cups (480ml) heavy cream
5 large egg yolks
1/2 cup (100g) granulated sugar
1 tsp vanilla extract
Pinch of salt
3 tbsp brown sugar (for caramelizing)

Directions:
Fill the Ninja Foodi possible cooker pro and preheat to 176°F (80°C) using the "sous vide" function.
In a bowl, whisk egg yolks, granulated sugar, vanilla extract, and a pinch of salt. Heat the cream until just beginning to simmer, then slowly whisk into the egg mixture.
Pour the mixture into sous vide-safe jars, seal, and submerge in the preheated water. Cook for 1-2 hours.
Chill the jars in an ice bath, then refrigerate for at least 4 hours or overnight. Sprinkle a thin, even layer of brown sugar on top and torch to caramelize just before serving.
Serve chilled with a crispy caramelized top.

NUTRITION Calories: 490 | Fat: 44g | Carbs: 13g | Protein: 32g

Sous Vide Tuna Steaks

Prep Time: 10 minutes
Cooking Time: 30-60 minutes
Serving: 2
Ingredients:
2 tuna steaks
2 tbsp soy sauce
1 tbsp honey
1 tbsp lemon juice
1 tsp minced garlic
1 tsp grated ginger
Salt and pepper to taste
Sesame seeds and green onions for garnish

Directions:
Fill the Ninja Foodi possible cooker pro and preheat to 122°F (50°C) for rare, 140°F (60°C) for medium.
In a bowl, mix soy sauce, honey, lemon juice, minced garlic, grated ginger, salt, and pepper.
Place tuna steaks in sous vide bags, pour the marinade over them, seal, and submerge in the preheated water. Cook for 30-60 minutes.
Remove the tuna from the bags and pat dry. Quickly sear in a hot skillet for a minute on each side.
Serve:
Garnish with sesame seeds and chopped green onions. Serve immediately.
NUTRITION Calories: 472 | Fat: 24g | Carbs: 13g | Protein: 53g

Sous Vide Beef Short Ribs

Prep Time: 20 minutes
Cooking Time: 24-48 hours
Serving: 4
Ingredients:
2 lbs (900g) beef short ribs
Salt and pepper to taste
2 sprigs fresh rosemary
4 cloves garlic, crushed
Olive oil for searing

Directions:
Fill the Ninja Foodi possible cooker pro and preheat to 140°F (60°C) using the "sous vide" function.
Season the short ribs with salt and pepper. Place them in a sous vide bag with rosemary and crushed garlic.
Seal the bag and submerge in the preheated water. Cook for 24-48 hours.
Remove the short ribs from the bag and pat dry. Sear in a hot skillet with olive oil for a minute on each side.
Serve with your preferred sides.
NUTRITION Calories: 890 | Fat: 44g | Carbs: 6g | Protein: 33g

Sous Vide Lamb Shanks

Prep Time: 20 minutes
Cooking Time: 24-48 hours
Serving: 2-4
Ingredients:
2 lamb shanks
Salt, pepper, and your choice of herbs/spices
Olive oil for searing

Directions:
Fill the Ninja Foodi possible cooker pro and preheat to 150°F (65.5°C) using the "sous vide" function.
Season the lamb shanks with salt, pepper, and your desired herbs/spices.
Place the lamb shanks in sous vide bags, seal, and submerge in the preheated water. Cook for 24-48 hours.
Remove the lamb shanks from the bags and pat dry. Sear in a hot skillet with olive oil for a minute on each side.
Serve with mashed potatoes or risotto.
NUTRITION Calories: 542 | Fat: 22g | Carbs: 3g | Protein: 64g

Sous Vide Chocolate Fondue

Prep Time: 10 minutes
Cooking Time: 1-2 hours
Serving: 4-6
Ingredients:
8 oz (225g) high-quality dark chocolate, chopped
1 cup (240ml) heavy cream
1 tsp vanilla extract
Assorted fruits and treats for dipping (e.g., strawberries, bananas, marshmallows)

Directions:
Fill the Ninja Foodi possible cooker pro and preheat to 131°F (55°C) using the "sous vide" function.
In a sous vide-safe container, combine the chopped chocolate, heavy cream, and vanilla extract.
Seal the container and submerge in the preheated water. Let it melt for 1-2 hours, gently stirring occasionally.
Once melted, carefully remove the container and serve the chocolate fondue with your favorite dippables.
NUTRITION Calories: 431 | Fat: 32g | Carbs: 39g | Protein: 4g

Sous Vide Lobster Tails

Prep Time: 10 minutes
Cooking Time: 30-60 minutes
Serving: 2
Ingredients:
2 lobster tails
Salt and pepper to taste
Butter, melted
Garlic, minced
Fresh parsley for garnish

Directions:
Fill the Ninja Foodi possible cooker pro and preheat to 140°F (60°C) using the "sous vide" function.
Split the lobster tails in half lengthwise. Season with salt and pepper.
Place the lobster tails in sous vide bags, drizzle with melted butter and minced garlic. Seal and submerge in the preheated water. Cook for 30-60 minutes.
Remove the lobster tails from the bags. Optionally, sear briefly in a hot skillet for color.
Garnish with fresh parsley and serve hot.

NUTRITION Calories: 220 | Fat: 11g | Carbs: 1g | Protein: 27g

Sous Vide Pulled Pork

Prep Time: 20 minutes
Cooking Time: 24-48 hours
Serving: 6-8
Ingredients:
4 lbs (1.8kg) pork shoulder or butt
Salt, pepper, and your favorite dry rub
Barbecue sauce

Directions:
Fill the Ninja Foodi possible cooker pro and preheat to 165°F (73.9°C) using the "sous vide" function.
Season the pork with salt, pepper, and your chosen dry rub. Place it in a sous vide bag.
Seal the bag and submerge in the preheated water. Cook for 24-48 hours.
Remove the pork from the bag and shred using forks. Mix with your favorite barbecue sauce.
Serve on buns as sandwiches.

NUTRITION Calories: 550 | Fat: 38g | Carbs: 4g | Protein: 49g

Sous Vide Veal Chops

Prep Time: 20 minutes
Cooking Time: 2-4 hours
Serving: 2
Ingredients:
2 veal chops
Salt and pepper to taste
Fresh thyme or rosemary
Olive oil for searing

Directions:
Fill the Ninja Foodi possible cooker pro and preheat to 140°F (60°C) using the "sous vide" function.
Season the veal chops with salt and pepper, and add fresh thyme or rosemary. Place them in a sous vide bag. Seal the bag and submerge in the preheated water. Cook for 2-4 hours.
Remove the veal chops from the bags and pat dry. Sear in a hot skillet with olive oil for a minute on each side. Serve with a side of your choice.

NUTRITION Calories: 570 | Fat: 35g | Carbs: 1g | Protein: 41g

Sous Vide Caramelized Onions

Prep Time: 10 minutes
Cooking Time: 12-24 hours
Serving: Varies
Ingredients:
4 large onions, thinly sliced
2 tbsp butter
Salt and sugar to taste

Directions:
Fill the Ninja Foodi possible cooker pro and preheat to 185°F (85°C) using the "sous vide" function.
In a sous vide-safe bag, combine the thinly sliced onions, butter, salt, and a pinch of sugar.
Seal the bag and submerge in the preheated water. Cook for 12-24 hours.
After sous vide, sauté the onions in a skillet over medium-high heat to caramelize.
Use caramelized onions as a topping for burgers, sandwiches, or salads.

NUTRITION Calories: 110 | Fat: 7g | Carbs: 12g | Protein: 1g

Sous Vide Meatballs

Prep Time: 20 minutes
Cooking Time: 1-2 hours
Serving: 4
Ingredients:
1 lb (450g) ground beef
1/2 cup breadcrumbs
1/4 cup grated Parmesan cheese
1 egg
Salt, pepper, and Italian seasoning to taste
Marinara sauce for serving

Directions:
Fill the Ninja Foodi possible cooker pro and preheat to 140°F (60°C) using the "sous vide" function.
In a bowl, mix ground beef, breadcrumbs, Parmesan cheese, egg, salt, pepper, and Italian seasoning until well combined.
Form the mixture into meatballs.
Place the meatballs in sous vide bags, seal, and submerge in the preheated water. Cook for 1-2 hours.
After sous vide, sear the meatballs in a hot skillet for a minute to brown the surface.
Serve the meatballs with marinara sauce.

NUTRITION Calories: 290 | **Fat:** 20g | **Carbs:** 6g | **Protein:** 22g

Sous Vide Apple Pie Filling

Prep Time: 15 minutes
Cooking Time: 2-4 hours
Serving: Varies
Ingredients:
4 cups (about 4-5) apples, peeled and sliced
1/2 cup (100g) brown sugar
1 tsp cinnamon
1/4 tsp nutmeg
1/4 tsp salt
2 tbsp butter

Directions:
Fill the Ninja Foodi possible cooker pro and preheat to 183°F (84°C) using the "sous vide" function.
In a bowl, combine apple slices, brown sugar, cinnamon, nutmeg, and salt. Mix well.
Place the mixture in a sous vide-safe bag, add butter, seal, and submerge in the preheated water. Cook for 2-4 hours.
Remove the bag from the water and let the filling cool.
Use the sous vide apple pie filling for pies, tarts, or as a topping for desserts.

NUTRITION Calories: 190 | **Fat:** 8g | **Carbs:** 32g | **Protein:** 4g

Sous Vide Corn on the Cob

Prep Time: 5 minutes
Cooking Time: 1-4 hours
Serving: 4
Ingredients:
4 ears of corn, husks removed
4 tbsp butter, melted
Salt and pepper to taste
Fresh parsley for garnish (optional)

Directions:
Fill the Ninja Foodi possible cooker pro and preheat to 183°F (84°C) using the "sous vide" function.
Brush each ear of corn with melted butter and season with salt and pepper. Place them in a sous vide bag.
Seal the bag and submerge in the preheated water. Cook for 1-4 hours.
Remove the corn from the bag and pat dry.
Garnish with fresh parsley if desired and serve.

NUTRITION Calories: 210 | **Fat:** 15g | **Carbs:** 22g | **Protein:** 3g

Sous Vide Infused Oils

Prep Time: 5 minutes
Cooking Time: 1-2 hours
Serving: Varies
Ingredients:
1 cup (240ml) olive oil
Herbs, garlic, or spices of your choice

Directions:
Fill the Ninja Foodi possible cooker pro and preheat to 140°F (60°C).
In a heatproof jar or bag, combine olive oil and your choice of herbs, garlic, or spices.
Seal the container and submerge in the preheated water. Infuse for 1-2 hours.
Strain the infused oil through a fine mesh strainer or cheesecloth. Store in a sealed container.
Use the infused oil for cooking, drizzling, or in dressings.

NUTRITION Calories: 140 | **Fat:** 19g | **Carbs:** 3g | **Protein:** 2g

Sous Vide Pulled Chicken

Prep Time: 15 minutes
Cooking Time: 4-6 hours
Serving: 4
Ingredients:
2 lbs (900g) boneless, skinless chicken breasts
1 cup barbecue sauce
1 tbsp brown sugar
1 tbsp smoked paprika
Salt and pepper to taste

Directions:
Fill the Ninja Foodi possible cooker pro and preheat to 140°F (60°C).
Sprinkle the chicken breasts with enough pepper, salt, and smoked paprika. Place them in a sous vide bag with barbecue sauce and brown sugar.
Seal the bag and submerge in the preheated water. Cook for 4-6 hrs.
Take out the chicken from the bag and shred using forks.
Toss the pulled chicken in additional barbecue sauce and serve in sandwiches or on its own.

NUTRITION Calories: 348 | Fat: 7g | Carbs: 24g | Protein: 34g

Sous Vide Cheesecake

Prep Time: 15 minutes
Cooking Time: 2-3 hours
Serving: 6
Ingredients:
2 (8-ounce) packages cream cheese, softened
1/2 cup (100g) granulated sugar
2 large eggs
1/4 cup (60ml) sour cream
1 tsp vanilla extract
Graham cracker crumbs and fruit for garnish

Directions:
Fill the Ninja Foodi possible cooker pro and preheat to 176°F (80°C) using the "sous vide" function.
In a clean bowl, combine the cheese and sugar until smooth.
Stir in sour cream, eggs, and vanilla extract, and mix until combined.
Divide the mixture into jars or containers suitable for sous vide. Seal and submerge in the preheated water. Cook for 2-3 hours.
Remove the jars and chill in the refrigerator for at least 4 hours or until set.
Garnish with graham cracker crumbs and your choice of fruit.

NUTRITION Calories: 380 | Fat: 21g | Carbs: 18g | Protein: 8g

CHAPTER NINE
PROOF RECIPES

Pizza Dough

Prep Time: 15 minutes
Cook Time: 1 hour (proofing time)
Servings: Makes 2 pizza doughs
Ingredients:
2 1/4 tsp active dry yeast
1 1/2 cups warm water (110°F/45°C)
1 tbsp sugar
3 1/2 - 4 cups all-purpose flour
2 tbsp olive oil
1 1/2 tsp salt

Directions:
In a small bowl, combine warm water and sugar. Stir to dissolve. Sprinkle yeast over the water and let it sit for about 5-10 minutes, until foamy.
In a large mixing bowl, combine flour and salt. Make a space in the center and add the activated yeast mixture and olive oil. Mix until a dough forms.
Knead the dough on a floured surface for about 10 minutes, or until smooth and elastic. Place in a greased bowl, cover with a damp cloth, and let it proof in the Ninja Foodi using the "proof" function for 1 hour or until doubled in size.
Preheat your oven or Ninja Foodi on the highest setting. Punch down the dough and divide it into two portions. Roll out each portion into a pizza crust of your desired thickness.
Add your favorite pizza toppings and bake in the preheated Ninja Foodi.

NUTRITION Calories: 291 | Fat: 3g | Carbs: 42g | Protein: 7g

Bread Rolls

Prep Time: 20 minutes
Cook Time: 30 minutes (proofing time included)
Servings: Makes 12 rolls
Ingredients:
1 1/4 cups warm milk
2 1/4 tsp active dry yeast
1/4 cup sugar
4 cups all-purpose flour
1/4 cup unsalted butter, melted
1 tsp salt

Directions:

In a clean bowl, combine milk and sugar. Stir to dissolve. Pour yeast over the milk and let it rest for about 5-10 minutes, until foamy.
In a clean bowl, combine flour and salt. Make a well in the center and add the activated yeast mixture and melted butter. Mix until a dough forms.
Knead the dough on a floured surface for about 10 minutes, or until smooth and elastic. Pour into a greased bowl, cover with a damp cloth, and let it proof in the Ninja Foodi using the "proof" function for 1-1.5 hours or until doubled in size.
Preheat your Ninja Foodi to 375°F (190°C).
Press down the dough and divide it into 12 portions. Shape each portion into a ball and place on a greased baking sheet.
Bake the bread rolls for 15-20 minutes or until the rolls are golden brown.

NUTRITION Calories: 233 | Fat: 4g | Carbs: 34g | Protein: 5.6g

Cinnamon Rolls

Prep Time: 30 minutes
Cook Time: 25 minutes (proofing time included)
Servings: Makes 12 cinnamon rolls
Ingredients:
1 batch of prepared Bread Roll dough (from the previous recipe)
1/3 cup unsalted butter, softened
1/2 cup brown sugar
2 tbsp ground cinnamon
For the glaze:
1 cup powdered sugar
2-3 tbsp milk
1/2 tsp vanilla extract

Directions:
After the bread dough has proofed, roll it out into a rectangle on a floured surface. Spread the butter over the dough, then add brown sugar and cinnamon evenly.
Roll the dough into a log and cut into 12 equal slices.
Put the cinnamon rolls in a greased baking dish and allow them proof using the "proof" function in the Ninja Foodi for 30 minutes.
Preheat your Ninja Foodi to 375°F (190°C) and bake the cinnamon rolls for 20-25 minutes or until golden brown.
In a clean bowl, combine sugar, milk, and vanilla extract to make the glaze. Drizzle over warm cinnamon rolls.

NUTRITION Calories: 355 | Fat: 13g | Carbs: 48g | Protein: 5g

Pretzels

Prep Time: 30 minutes
Cook Time: 15 minutes (proofing time included)
Servings: Makes 8 pretzels
Ingredients:
1 batch of prepared Bread Roll dough (from the previous recipe)
10 cups water
2/3 cup baking soda
Coarse salt for sprinkling

Directions:
Preheat your Ninja Foodi to 450°F (230°C).
Divide the bread dough into 8 equal portions and roll each portion to form a long rope. Shape each rope into a pretzel.
In a clean pot, boil 10 cups of water. Add the baking soda and let it dissolve.
Carefully place each pretzel into the boiling water for about 30 seconds, then remove and place on a baking sheet.
Sprinkle the pretzels with salt and bake in the preheated Ninja Foodi for 12-15 minutes or until golden brown.

NUTRITION Calories: 246 | Fat: 1g | Carbs: 49g | Protein: 8g

Bagels

Prep Time: 30 minutes
Cook Time: 25 minutes (proofing time included)
Servings: Makes 8 bagels
Ingredients:
1 batch of prepared Bread Roll dough (from the previous recipe)
1 egg, beaten (for egg wash)
Sesame seeds, poppy seeds, or other toppings of choice

Directions:
Preheat your Ninja Foodi to 400°F (200°C). Divide the bread dough into 8 equal portions and shape each portion into a ball.
Flatten the balls and make a hole in the center, then shape into a bagel.
Place the bagels on a baking sheet and let them proof using the "proof" function in the Ninja Foodi for 20-25 minutes.
Brush the tops of the bagels with whisked egg and add your choice of toppings.
Bake in the preheated Ninja Foodi for 20-25 minutes or until golden brown.

NUTRITION Calories: 267 | Fat: 2g | Carbs: 44g | Protein: 7g

Focaccia

Prep Time: 20 minutes
Cook Time: 30 minutes (proofing time included)
Servings: Makes one 9x13-inch focaccia
Ingredients:
1 batch of prepared Bread Roll dough (from the previous recipe)
1/4 cup olive oil
1 tbsp rosemary leaves
Coarse sea salt

Directions:
Preheat your Ninja Foodi to 400°F (200°C).
Grease a 9x13-inch baking pan and press the dough into the pan.
Pour olive oil over the dough and sprinkle with rosemary leaves and coarse sea salt.
Let it proof using the "proof" function in the Ninja Foodi for 30 minutes.
Bake in the preheated Ninja Foodi for 25-30 minutes or until golden brown.

NUTRITION Calories: 242 | Fat: 7g | Carbs: 33g | Protein: 7g

Dinner Rolls

Prep Time: 20 minutes
Cook Time: 20 minutes (proofing time included)
Servings: Makes 12 dinner rolls
Ingredients:
1 batch of prepared Bread Roll dough (from the previous recipe)
2 tbsp unsalted butter, melted

Directions:
Preheat your Ninja Foodi to 375°F (190°C). Divide the dinner rolls dough into 12 equal portions and shape each into a ball.
Place the dinner rolls in a greased baking dish and let them proof using the "proof" function in the Ninja Foodi for 30 minutes.
Brush the tops of the dinner rolls with melted butter.
Bake in the preheated Ninja Foodi for 18-20 minutes or until golden brown.

NUTRITION Calories: 189 | Fat: 3g | Carbs: 35g | Protein: 5g

Croissants

Prep Time: 30 minutes
Cook Time: 20 minutes (proofing time included)
Servings: Makes 12 croissants
Ingredients:
1 batch of prepared Bread Roll dough (from the previous recipe)
1/2 cup unsalted butter, softened
Egg wash (1 egg beaten with a splash of water)

Directions:
Preheat your Ninja Foodi to 375°F (190°C). Roll out the dough on a floured surface to about 1/4-inch thickness.
Spread softened butter over the dough.
Cut the croissant dough into triangles and roll each triangle into a croissant shape.
Place the croissants on a baking sheet and let them proof using the "proof" function in the Ninja Foodi for 30 minutes.
Brush the croissants with the egg wash.
Bake in the preheated oven or Ninja Foodi for 15-20 minutes or until golden brown.
NUTRITION Calories: 308 | Fat: 16g | Carbs: 34g | Protein: 6g

Hot Cross Buns

Prep Time: 30 minutes
Cook Time: 25 minutes (proofing time included)
Servings: Makes 12 buns
Ingredients:
1 batch of prepared Bread Roll dough (from the previous recipe)
1/4 cup raisins or currants
1/4 cup candied peel (optional)
1 tsp ground cinnamon
1/4 tsp ground nutmeg
For the cross:
1/2 cup all-purpose flour
1/4 cup water
For the glaze:
1/4 cup apricot jam or jelly, heated

Directions:
Preheat your Ninja Foodi to 375°F (190°C). Mix the raisins, candied peel, cinnamon, and nutmeg into the dough.
Divide the buns dough into 12 equal portions and shape each into a bun.
Place the buns on a baking sheet and let them proof using the "proof" function in the Ninja Foodi for 30 minutes.

For the cross, mix flour and water to form a thick paste. Pipe crosses onto the buns.
Bake in the preheated oven or Ninja Foodi for 20-25 minutes or until golden brown.
Brush the buns with heated apricot jam for a glaze.

NUTRITION Calories: 229 | Fat: 4g | Carbs: 43g | Protein: 4g

Sourdough Bread

Prep Time: 15 minutes (+ sourdough starter preparation)
Cook Time: 40 minutes (proofing time included)
Servings: Makes 1 loaf
Ingredients:
1 cup sourdough starter
1 1/2 cups warm water
4 cups bread flour
1 1/2 tsp salt

Directions:
Combine sourdough starter, water, and 3 cups of flour in a clean bowl. Mix well and let it sit for 30 minutes.
Add salt and the remaining flour gradually, mixing until a dough forms.
Knead the dough on a floured surface for about 10 minutes until smooth and elastic.
Place the dough in a greased container, cover with a damp cloth, and allow to proof using the "proof" function in the Ninja Foodi for 6-8 hrs or until doubled in size. Preheat your Ninja Foodi to 450°F.
Transfer the dough to the preheated Ninja Foodi, cover, and bake for 30 mins.
Bake for an additional 10-15 minutes or until the crust is golden brown.
NUTRITION Calories: 227 | Fat: 1g | Carbs: 47g | Protein: 6g

Naan

Prep Time: 15 minutes
Cook Time: 10 minutes (proofing time included)
Servings: Makes 6 naans
Ingredients:
2 1/2 cups all-purpose flour
1 tsp sugar
1 tsp baking powder
1/4 cup yogurt
3/4 cup warm water
2 tbsp olive oil
Butter for brushing
Optional: garlic, chopped coriander for topping

Directions:
In a clean bowl, combine water, sugar, and yeast. Let it sit for about 10 minutes until frothy.
In a clean mixing bowl, mix the yogurt, flour, baking powder, and the yeast mixture. Mix well.
Knead the dough for about 5-7 minutes until smooth.
Put in a greased bowl, cover with a damp cloth, and let it proof using the "proof" function in the Ninja Foodi for 1-2 hours or until doubled in size.
Preheat your Ninja Foodi "bake" function to the highest setting.
Divide the naan dough into 6 portions and roll each into an oval shape.
Cook each naan for about 1-2 minutes on each side in a preheated skillet or on the griddle function in the Ninja Foodi until puffed and lightly browned.
Brush with butter and sprinkle with garlic and chopped coriander if desired.
NUTRITION Calories: 298 | Fat: 7g | Carbs: 40g | Protein: 7g

Flatbread

Prep Time: 15 minutes
Cook Time: 15 minutes (proofing time included)
Servings: Makes 8 flatbreads
Ingredients:
2 1/2 cups all-purpose flour
1 tsp salt
1 cup warm water
2 tbsp olive oil

Directions:
In a clean bowl, combine flour and salt. Gradually add warm water and olive oil, mixing until a dough forms. Knead the dough for about 5 minutes until smooth. Put it in a greased bowl, cover with a damp cloth, and let it proof using the "proof" function in the Ninja Foodi for 1 hour or until doubled in size.
Preheat your oven or Ninja Foodi to 400°F (200°C).

Divide the flatbread dough into 8 equal portions and roll each portion into a round flatbread.
Cook each flatbread on a hot skillet or on the griddle function in the Ninja Foodi for about 2-3 minutes on each side or until lightly golden and puffed.
NUTRITION Calories: 228 | Fat: 9.4g | Carbs: 31g | Protein: 7.2g

Brioche

Prep Time: 30 minutes
Cook Time: 30 minutes (proofing time included)
Servings: Makes 1 brioche loaf
Ingredients:
3 1/4 cups all-purpose flour
1/4 cup sugar
1 tbsp active dry yeast
1/2 cup warm milk
3 large eggs
1/2 cup unsalted butter, softened
1 tsp salt

Directions:
In a clean bowl, mix milk and sugar together. Stir to dissolve. Spread yeast over the milk and let it sit for about 5-10 minutes, until foamy.
In a clean bowl, combine flour and salt. Make a well in the center and add the activated yeast mixture, eggs, and softened butter. Mix until a dough forms. Knead the dough on a floured surface for about 10-15 minutes, or until smooth and elastic. Place in a greased bowl, cover with a damp cloth, and let it proof using the "proof" function in the Ninja Foodi for 1-1.5 hours or until doubled in size.
Preheat your oven or Ninja Foodi to 375°F (190°C). Shape the Brioche dough into a loaf and place it in a greased loaf pan.
Bake in the preheated oven or Ninja Foodi for 25-30 minutes or until golden brown.

NUTRITION Calories: 423 | Fat: 11g | Carbs: 23g | Protein: 7g

English Muffins

Prep Time: 30 minutes
Cook Time: 20 minutes (proofing time included)
Servings: Makes 12 muffins
Ingredients:
4 1/2 cups all-purpose flour
1 tbsp sugar
1 1/2 tsp salt
1 1/2 tsp active dry yeast
1 1/4 cups warm milk
2 tbsp unsalted butter, melted
Cornmeal for dusting

Directions:
In a bowl, combine warm milk and sugar. Stir to dissolve. Spread yeast over the milk and let it sit for about 5-10 minutes, until foamy.
In a clean bowl, combine flour and salt. Make a well in the center and add the activated yeast mixture and melted butter. Mix until a dough forms.
Knead the dough on a floured surface for about 10-15 minutes, or until smooth and elastic. Place in a greased bowl, cover with a damp cloth, and let it proof using the "proof" function in the Ninja Foodi for 1-1.5 hours or until doubled in size.
Preheat a skillet over medium heat.
Roll out the muffins dough to about 1/2-inch thickness and cut into rounds using a biscuit cutter.
Sprinkle the skillet or griddle with cornmeal and cook the muffins for about 5-7 minutes on each side or until lightly golden.

NUTRITION Calories: 167 | **Fat:** 2g | **Carbs:** 33g | **Protein:** 4g

Challah

Prep Time: 30 minutes
Cook Time: 30 minutes (proofing time included)
Servings: Makes 1 loaf
Ingredients:
4 1/2 cups all-purpose flour
1/2 cup sugar
1 1/2 tsp salt
1 1/2 tsp active dry yeast
1/2 cup warm water
4 large eggs, lightly beaten
1/2 cup vegetable oil

Directions:
In a bowl, combine water and 1 tablespoon of sugar. Stir to dissolve. Sprinkle yeast over the water and let it sit for about 5-10 minutes, until foamy.

In a clean bowl, combine flour, remaining sugar, and salt. Make a well in the center and add the activated yeast mixture, beaten eggs, and vegetable oil. Mix until a dough forms.
Knead the dough on a floured surface for about 10-15 minutes, or until smooth and elastic. Place in a greased bowl, cover with a damp cloth, and let it proof using the "proof" function in the Ninja Foodi for 1-1.5 hours or until doubled in size.
Preheat your oven or Ninja Foodi to 375°F (190°C). Divide the Challah dough into three equal portions and braid them together to form the challah. Place in a greased loaf pan.
Bake in the preheated oven or Ninja Foodi for 25-30 minutes or until golden brown.

NUTRITION Calories: 297 | **Fat:** 12g | **Carbs:** 31g | **Protein:** 8g

Whole Wheat Bread

Prep Time: 20 minutes
Cook Time: 30 minutes (proofing time included)
Servings: Makes 1 loaf
Ingredients:
2 1/2 cups whole wheat flour
1 1/4 cups warm water
2 tbsp honey
1 packet (2 1/4 tsp) active dry yeast
2 tbsp olive oil
1 tsp salt

Directions:
In a small bowl, combine warm water and honey. Stir to dissolve. Sprinkle yeast over the water and let it sit for about 5-10 minutes, until foamy.
In a clean bowl, combine whole wheat flour and salt. Make a well in the center and add the activated yeast mixture and olive oil. Mix until a dough forms. Knead the dough on a floured surface for about 10-15 minutes, or until smooth and elastic. Place in a greased bowl, cover with a damp cloth, and let it proof using the "proof" function in the Ninja Foodi for 1-1.5 hours or until doubled in size.
Preheat your oven or Ninja Foodi to 375°F (190°C). Shape the Bread dough into a loaf and place it in a greased loaf pan.
Bake in the preheated oven or Ninja Foodi for 25-30 minutes or until golden brown.

NUTRITION Calories: 128 | **Fat:** 3g | **Carbs:** 21g | **Protein:** 4g

French Bread

Prep Time: 20 minutes
Cook Time: 25 minutes (proofing time included)
Servings: Makes 2 loaves
Ingredients:
4 cups bread flour
1 1/2 cups warm water
2 tsp active dry yeast
1 1/2 tsp salt

Directions:
In a clean bowl, combin water and yeast. Stir to dissolve. Let it sit for about 5-10 minutes, until foamy.
In a clean bowl, combine bread flour and salt. Make a well in the center and add the activated yeast mixture. Mix until a dough forms.
Knead the dough on a floured surface for about 10-15 minutes or until smooth and elastic. Place in a greased bowl, cover with a damp cloth, and let it proof using the "proof" function in the Ninja Foodi for 1-1.5 hours or until doubled in size.
Preheat your Ninja Foodi using the "bake" function to 450°F (230°C).
Divide the dough in half and shape each half into a long loaf. Place on a baking sheet.
Make diagonal slashes on the top of each loaf with a sharp knife.
Bake in the preheated Ninja Foodi for 20-25 minutes or until golden brown.

NUTRITION Calories: 146 | Fat: 1g | Carbs: 30g | Protein: 4g

Cranberry Orange Bread

Prep Time: 20 minutes
Cook Time: 55 minutes (proofing time included)
Servings: Makes 1 loaf
Ingredients:
2 cups all-purpose flour
1/2 cup sugar
1 1/2 tsp baking powder
1/2 tsp baking soda
1/2 tsp salt
1/2 cup orange juice
Zest of 1 orange
1/4 cup unsalted butter, melted
1 large egg
1 cup fresh cranberries
Directions:

Preheat your Ninja Foodi to 350°F (175°C) using the "bake" function. Grease and flour a loaf pan.
In a clean bowl, combine sugar, baking powder, flour, baking soda, and salt.
In another bowl, mix orange juice, orange zest, melted butter, and egg.
Mix both wet and dry ingredients together. Fold in the cranberries.
Pour the mixture into the available loaf pan and let it proof using the "proof" function in the Ninja Foodi for 30-40 minutes.
Bake in the preheated Ninja Foodi for 50-55 mins.

NUTRITION Calories: 244 | Fat: 7g | Carbs: 28g | Protein: 4g

Pita Bread

Prep Time: 20 minutes
Cook Time: 5 minutes (proofing time included)
Servings: Makes 8 pitas
Ingredients:
3 cups all-purpose flour
1 1/4 cups warm water
1 tsp sugar
1 packet (2 1/4 tsp) active dry yeast
1 1/2 tsp salt
1 tbsp olive oil

Directions:
In a small bowl, combine warm water and sugar. Stir to dissolve. Sprinkle yeast over the water and let it sit for about 5-10 minutes, until foamy.
In a clean bowl, combine flour and salt. Make a well in the center and add the activated yeast mixture and olive oil. Mix until a dough forms.
Knead the dough on a floured surface for about 5 minutes or until smooth and elastic. Place in a greased bowl, cover with a damp cloth, and let it proof using the "proof" function in the Ninja Foodi for 1 hour or until doubled in size.
Preheat a skillet over medium-high heat. Divide the pita bread dough into 8 equal portions and roll into a ball. Roll out each pita bread ball into a circle about 1/4-inch thick.
Cook each pita for about 1-2 minutes on each side on the skillet or griddle until puffed and lightly browned.

NUTRITION Calories: 197 | Fat: 2g | Carbs: 29g | Protein: 5g

CHAPTER TEN

KEEP WARM FUNCTION

As explained in Chapter One, using the "Keep Warm" function on the Ninja Foodi Possible Cooker Pro is a simple process that helps maintain the temperature of your cooked food at a safe and serving-ready level.

Here are the steps on how to use this function:

STEP ONE: Cook Your Dish

Start by cooking your dish using one of the appropriate cooking functions, such as slow cook, proof, saute/sear, braise, bake, or any other method that requires your desired cooking time and temperature.

STEP TWO: Finish Cooking

Once your dish has finished cooking, make sure the appliance is still plugged in and turned on. Most Ninja Foodi possible cooker pro models will automatically switch to the "Keep Warm" function once the cooking cycle is complete, but you may need to manually select it on some models.

STEP THREE: Select the "Keep Warm" Function (if needed)

If your appliance doesn't automatically switch to the "Keep Warm" function, you can manually select it on the control panel. Look for a button or setting labeled "Keep Warm" or a similar option. Press it to activate the function.

STEP FOUR: Adjust Settings (if necessary)

Depending on the model of your Ninja Foodi, you may be able to adjust the "Keep Warm" settings, such as the temperature or the duration for which you want to keep your food warm. Refer to your user manual for specific instructions on adjusting these settings.

STEP FIVE: Keep the Lid Closed

To maintain the proper temperature and prevent heat loss, keep the appliance's lid closed while using the "Keep Warm" function. This also helps prevent moisture from escaping, keeping your food from drying out.

STEP SIX: Serve When Ready

Your dish will now be kept at a safe and serving-ready temperature, allowing you to serve it whenever you and your guests are ready to eat. Be sure to use oven mitts or heat-resistant gloves when handling hot components.

STEP SEVEN: Check Food Temperature (if needed)

If you're serving a dish that requires a specific temperature for food safety reasons (e.g., poultry), use a food thermometer to ensure it remains within the safe temperature range throughout the "Keep Warm" period.

STEP EIGHT: Turn Off "Keep Warm" When Done

When you're finished serving or if you want to stop using the "Keep Warm" function, simply press the "Keep Warm" button again (if manually activated) or follow your user manual's instructions to turn off the function.

STEP NINE: Unplug the Appliance

To ensure safety and energy conservation, unplug the appliance when you're finished using it or when you don't intend to use it for an extended period.

NINJA FOODI POSSIBLE COOKER PRO MEASUREMENT CONVERSION TABLE

Volume Equivalents (Liquid)

US STANDARD	METRIC (APPROXIMATE)	US STANDARD (OUNCES)
2 tablespoons	30 mL	1 fl. oz.
¼ cup	60 mL	2 fl. oz.
½ cup	120 mL	4 fl. oz.
1 cup	240 mL	8 fl. oz.
1½ cups	355 mL	12 fl. oz.
2 cups or 1 pint	475 mL	16 fl. oz.
4 cups or 1 quart	1 L	32 fl. oz.
1 gallon	4 L	128 fl. oz.

Ninja Foodi Possible Cooker Pro Temperatures

FAHRENHEIT (F)	CELSIUS (C) (APPROXIMATE)
250°	120°
300°	150°
325°	165°
350°	180°
375°	190°
400°	200°
425°	220°
450°	230°

Weight Equivalent

US STANDARD	METRIC (APPROXIMATE)
½ ounce	15 g
1 ounce	30 g
2 ounces	60 g
4 ounces	115 g
8 ounces	225 g
12 ounces	340 g
16 ounces or 1 pound	455 g

Volume Equivalents (Dry)

US STANDARD	METRIC (APPROXIMATE)
⅛ teaspoon	0.5 mL
¼ teaspoon	1 mL
½ teaspoon	2 mL
¾ teaspoon	4 mL
1 teaspoon	5 mL
1 tablespoon	15 mL
¼ cup	59 mL
⅓ cup	79 mL
½ cup	118 mL
⅔ cup	156 mL
¾ cup	177 mL
1 cup	235 mL
2 cups or 1 pint	475 mL
3 cups	700 mL
4 cups or 1 quart	1 L

CONCLUSION

I hope you've enjoyed this cookbook and learned a lot about your Ninja Foodi Possible Cooker Pro. This versatile appliance can do it all, from slow cooking to sous vide, and I hope you have found some new recipes to try.

Don't be afraid to experiment with different recipes and cooking times. With a little practice, you'll be able to master all of the different functions of your Ninja Foodi Possible Cooker Pro. Also, read the user manual carefully before using your cooker. This will help you understand how to use all the different functions and settings.

And remember, the Ninja Foodi Possible Cooker Pro is more than just a kitchen appliance. It's a tool that can help you save time, eat healthier, and have more fun in the kitchen.

The possibilities are endless!

INDEX OF RECIPES

Made in the USA
Las Vegas, NV
10 February 2025

17841712R00050